Harnessing Global Value Chains for regional development

How to upgrade through regional policy, FDI and trade

RICCARDO CRESCENZI AND OLIVER HARMAN

Regional Studies Policy Impact Books
Series Editor: Louise Kempton

T0313096

Regional Studies
Association
Research Today, Policy Tomorrow

DIRECTED BY

First published 2023
by Taylor & Francis
4 Park Square, Milton Park, Abingdon, Oxon, OX14 4RN

Taylor & Francis Group, an informa business

British Library Cataloguing-in-Publication Data
A catalogue record for this book is available from the British Library.

Trademark notice: Product or corporate names may be trademarks or registered trademarks, and are used only for identification and explanation without intent to infringe.

ISBN13: 978-1-032-41076-0 (print)
ISBN13: 978-1-003-35614-1 (e-book)

Typeset in 10.5/13.5 Myriad Pro
by Nova Techset Private Limited, Bengaluru and Chennai, India

Disclosure statement: No potential conflict of interest was reported by the authors.

Please visit https://taylorandfrancis.com/about/corporate-responsibility/accessibility-at-taylor-francis/ for further information on the accessibility features available for Regional Studies Policy Impact Books

CONTENTS

Harnessing Global Value Chains for regional development:

How to upgrade through regional policy, FDI and trade

Academic foreword	1
Policy foreword I	3
Policy foreword II	5
About the authors	7
Acknowledgments	9
Frequent abbreviations	11
The book in a nutshell	13
1. Introduction	21
2. **Why do GVCs matter for regions: key concepts, definitions and trends**	27
2.1 The importance of global value chains	29
2.2 The governance of GVCs and the role of multinational enterprises	35
2.3 The significance of foreign direct investment for GVCs and their localisation	38
2.4 The role of subnational regions in GVC and FDI	41
2.5 Changing the perspective—old paradigm versus new paradigm	46
2.6 Regional upgrading	48
3. How to upgrade through regional policy: building GVCs through FDI	57
3.1 What is driving MNE decision-making and how can subnational policy attract their cross-border activities?	59
3.2 What factors matter for attracting GVC investment flows?	61
3.3 Varying drivers of location choice	63

4. How to upgrade through regional policy: embedding GVCs through FDI   **69**

4.1   Technology diffusion and innovation in host region   72

4.2   Can firms offshoring investment abroad help home regions?   74

4.3   Varying drivers of impact   77

5. How to upgrade through regional policy: reshaping GVCs through FDI   **85**

5.1   Regional leadership   88

5.2   A diagnostic tool: GVC Mapping and analysis   91

5.3   A regional policy: investment promotion agencies and local content units   93

6. Looking to the future and useful tools for leveraging GVCs   **105**

6.1   GVCs and the digital transition: automation, artificial intelligence and digital work practices   108

6.2   Green GVCs and the green transition   110

6.3   Data and intelligence to navigate change   112

6.4   Final remarks   113

Figures and boxes

Box 2.1	The smiling curve of value added	30
Figure 2.1	The rise of global value chains	31
Figure 2.2	GVCs and MNEs	34
Figure 2.3	GVCs, MNEs, and the regional economy	35
Figure 2.4	Horizontal and vertical MNE linkages	37
Figure 2.5	How FDI links global values chains (GVCs) and regions	40
Figure 2.6	Maps of FDI (a) inflow and (b) outflow by region, 2003–17	42
Figure 2.7	Old versus new paradigm in regional development	47
Figure 4.1	Knowledge benefits of outsourcing	71
Figure 5.1	Role of IPAs and LCUs in generating impact from GVC investment	98

Case studies

Case study 1.	Non-patent regional upgrading and innovation in Torreón, Mexico	49
Case study 2.	Penang Skills Development Centre (PSDC), Malaysia	63
Case study 3.	Local embedding of firms in Istanbul, Turkey	72
Case study 4.	Knowledge benefits of offshoring—CEMEX, Mexico	76
Case study 5.	Removing upgrading bottlenecks in Emilia-Romagna, Italy, and Antigua, Guatemala	91
Case study 6.	Subnational IPAs, North Middle Sweden	95
Case study 7.	Linkages programmes in Ireland and Singapore	97
Case study 8.	Firm mapping in Costa Rica	97

Academic foreword

Global value chains (GVCs) have a central role in the international economy. They have shown remarkable resilience in confronting major global disruptions such as Covid-19 and the war in Ukraine. The configuration of GVCs has evolved over time along with the participation and position of different countries in the global economy. However, a large body of empirical evidence has consistently shown a positive link between GVC engagement and economic progress. On balance, the global fragmentation of production has generated new windows of opportunity for development. Whether and how these openings can be harnessed for development have become prominent questions for academics and policymakers alike.

These questions and their answers underpin the evidence upon which this book is based. A main focus is the academic literature providing the historical foundations and cutting-edge research on public policies for GVCs and development. For this reason alone, the book is worth your time. Beyond this, this book makes four additional contributions to our understanding of the local impacts of economic globalisation:

1) It adds a subnational or regional lens to much of the literature. As indicated in the text, all GVCs touch down in space—whether it be a city, region or industrial cluster. This connection with the local socio-economic context is often lacking in research on GVCs, which can be perceived as unwieldy concepts rather than potential drivers of change for citizens. The adoption of this lens fills this important gap.

2) It illustrates concretely how foreign direct investment (FDI) can drive the process of upgrading—particularly through its ability to transfer knowledge. By positioning FDI motives, location choices and outcomes within the wider GVC framework, the book offers a new perspective to understand and shape local impacts. For example, through the GVC lens, the discussion of the potential regional benefits of outward FDI—in addition to the well-known merits of inward FDI—brings a new perspective to the role of these global investment flows. Engaging with FDI

https://
doi.org/10.1080/2578711X.2022.2099151 ©
2023 Riccardo Crescenzi and Oliver Harman

in the ways outlined in the book offers new scripts for policymakers to drive constructive local economic development.

3) It directly engages with the dynamic contexts of GVC engagement. The work highlights variations in regional assets and firm motives, revealing a process of building, embedding and reshaping GVCs depending on the local setting. This notion of development as discovery is core to the upgrading story, ensuring economies do not stay stationery and risk becoming locked into traditional development trajectories.

4) It suggests pathways to link GVCs with an evidence-based evaluation of public policies. Readers are presented with solid information on what works (and what does not) in practice, which could provide new insights for how to design and evaluate research that could spur the policy-evaluation literature.

For readers and researchers, this publication could not be timelier. Long-term trends such as automation, digitisation and climate change are intersecting with more recent disruptions such as Covid-19, backshoring of production and raw geopolitical conflicts. These will influence GVCs in multiple and uncharted ways. Challenges within the global economy cannot be reduced to ideological talking points. We need more research on how to harness GVCs for regional development, given the well-known data limitations that fuel both knowledge gaps and policy gaps. Hopefully, this book can help to motivate and improve future studies and provide policy decision-makers with additional tools and evidence to confront this uncertainty.

Echoing a key theme from some of my earlier work, it is *a not only a matter of whether to participate in the global economy, but how to do so gainfully.* This policy impact book brings us closer to this reality.

Gary Gereffi
Emeritus Professor of Sociology and Director of the Global Value Chains Center, Duke University, Durham, NC, USA
ggereffi@duke.edu

https://doi.org/10.1080/2578711X.2022.2099151

Policy foreword I

Considering regions as purely "local" economies overlooks opportunities and threats from global connectivity. Tradable sectors are essential for regional development. First, the less dense and remote regions are actually obliged to specialise in tradables. They do not benefit from agglomeration economies and so it is not easy to develop services (except perhaps public services). Second, there is evidence from the Organisation for Economic Co-operation and Development's (OECD) work that regional productivity catching-up is associated with the presence of tradable sectors. They support "unconditional" productivity convergence, which is key in the presence of weaker institutional basis and capacity. Third, in a globalised world, sustaining specialisation in tradable sectors means being connected to global value chains (GVCs). Depending on the estimates, 60–80% of global trade flows are directly or indirectly related to the activities of multinational enterprises.

These facts stress the importance of this book, for both European national and regional policy-makers. It provides analysis and guidelines to help them formulate strategies for international connectivity, navigate the negotiations with global companies and make the most out of regional/local strengths. International companies are typically very sensitive to local conditions and spatial arbitrages for the choice and location of their investments. In this context, policymakers need to be equipped with a good understanding of what the region has to offer and the kind of opportunities generated by foreign direct investments.

Accordingly, key actors are placing GVCs and global connectivity at the centre stage of policy. The European Union's Cohesion Policy, the World Bank, the Asian Investment Bank and the African Union are devoting efforts to the subject. While of a key interest for policy, the book is also of utmost interest to students and scholars alike focusing on a rigorous discussion of this emerging topic, which has been rarely analysed at the regional level.

At the OECD, I had the opportunity to follow the conception of this work. Its development and iteration, through dialogue with academics and policymakers alike, has only further

https://
doi.org/10.1080/2578711X.2022.2099153 ©
2023 Riccardo Crescenzi and Oliver Harman

strengthened its relevance. It is a fine piece of empirical research that provides sound ground for policy implementation. A main message is that we must change the paradigm upon which we view policy on GVCs. It is not enough to be open. GVCs do matter, but they should be leveraged for regional innovation and upgrading.

In the aftermath of Covid-19 and with rising global insecurity, many decision-makers readdress value chains and want to redefine globalisation strategies for their countries and regions. This book is a timely and critical contribution to this debate.

Joaquim Oliveira Martins
Special Advisor to the European Union Commissioner for Cohesion and Reforms
Counsellor, Centre for Prospective Studies and International Information, Paris, France
Lecturer, PSL—University Paris Dauphine, Paris, France
joaquim.oliveira@cepii.fr

Policy foreword II

Reading through the book's contents has been an "Aha!" experience for me. It feels like finally the pieces in the puzzle of moving subnational/regional development to the next level are being handed to us, particularly so as leaders in Africa.

Having for such a long time basically muted and even ignored the existing advantages, resources and technology that have become part of our fabric, we have sought solutions and resources, developed in and for other contexts, often with disappointing outcomes.

The book invites the regional leaders who are also policymakers to identify, appraise and appreciate the innovation, capabilities, opportunities and potential of where they are situated and identify global value chains (GVCs) and foreign direct investment (FDI) that they will work with to harness their capabilities and best advantage to spur regional development.

The book zooms into practical ways in which regions can identify and forge strong and equitable partnerships with international chains to access international markets without the traditional west to south connotations. It also shares how to lift the economic well-being of the people they host.

The authors make useful suggestions of a unique needs-specific approach to policy formulation. Policies are made to enable and take advantage of those GVCs and FDI networks that provide the best advantage to the regions, away from the usual route of policy first, then trying to fit partners and strategies into them—leading to misfits and frustration to long-term development.

Leaders, especially in developing economies, will now have a choice of how best to drive their development based on existing strengths innovations and resources. The new symbiotic

https://
doi.org/10.1080/2578711X.2022.2099154 ©
2023 Riccardo Crescenzi and Oliver Harman

relationships with GVCs and FDIs will be more focused, more beneficial to both, and deliver longer term, more sustainable development in regions.

The book is a gem!

Jennifer Musisi

First City Leader in Residence, Bloomberg Harvard City Leadership Initiative,
Harvard University, Cambridge, MA, USA
Senior Policy Advisor, International Growth Centre and Council Member,
Cities that Work Council
Member of Board of Directors, C40 Cities
UN Ambassador for Sustainable Development, SDG 11
Council Member, Global Future Council on Cities of Tomorrow, World Economic Forum
Former Executive Director of Kampala Capital City Authority, Kampala, Uganda

https://doi.org/10.1080/2578711X.2022.2099154

About the authors

Riccardo Crescenzi is a Professor of Economic Geography at the London School of Economics and Political Science (LSE), UK.

He has been a European Research Council (ERC) grant holder, leading a major five-year research project on foreign direct investment (FDI), global value chains (GVCs) and their territorial impacts across the globe. He is currently the LSE Principal Investigator of a large collaborative research project funded by Horizon Europe and UK Research and Innovation (UKRI) on inequalities in the era of global megatrends.

Riccardo has been a Jean Monnet Fellow at the European University Institute (EUI), a Visiting Scholar at the Taubman Centre at Harvard University, and at the University of California—Los Angeles (UCLA), as well as an Associate at the Centre for International Development (CID) at the Harvard Kennedy School of Government.

He has provided academic advice to, amongst others, the European Investment Bank (EIB), the European Parliament, the European Commission, the Inter-American Investment Bank (IADB), the Asian Infrastructure Investment Bank (AIIB), the Organisation for Economic Co-operation and Development (OECD) and the World Bank. Riccardo has also served as the Rapporteur of the High-Level Expert Group on Innovative Cities established by the European Commissioner for Research and Innovation and has been part of the National Commission for Infrastructure and Sustainable Mobility established by the Italian Government to plan investment in sustainable mobility until 2050.

He has a long track-record of teaching and research in regional economic development, innovation, FDI and GVCs, and in the analysis and evaluation of public policies. This research is published in top peer-reviewed journals in economic geography, international economics and international business and management and widely cited in academic and policy circles.

✉ r.crescenzi@lse.ac.uk ⓘ 0000-0003-0465-9796

https://
doi.org/10.1080/2578711X.2022.2099157 ©
2023 Riccardo Crescenzi and Oliver Harman

Oliver Harman is a Cities Economist for the International Growth Centre's (IGC) Cities that Work initiative based at the Blavatnik School of Government, University of Oxford, UK, and Associate Staff at the London School of Economics and Political Science (LSE), UK. He is also a Clarendon Scholar studying the multilevel governance and financing of sustainable urban development in low-income and fast-growing cities. In these roles he attempts to help bridge the gap between research and policy, both generating and translating economic literature into clear urban policy guidance for emerging country city governments.

Oliver engages with local government ministries and mayoral teams primarily across West, Central and East Africa, as well as South Asia. His three thematic interests include financing sustainable urban development, global value chains (GVCs) for regional upgrading and climate change in cities.

✉ oliver.harman@bsg.ox.ac.uk ⓘ 0000-0001-7459-1470

Acknowledgments

An earlier version of this manuscript was prepared as a background document for an Organisation for Economic Co-operation and Development (OECD) Workshop on "Broadening Innovation Policy—New Insights for Regions and Cities", which received funding from the European Union. The manuscript was improved by very helpful feedback and discussion with Rudiger Ahrend, Peter Berkowitz, Alexander Lembcke, Ana Novik, Joaquim Oliveira Martins and Annalisa Primi, as well as David Bailey, Matija Rojec and Vincent Vicard.

The authors thank the OECD for authorisation to publish the updated manuscript in this form. The content of which is the sole responsibility of the authors and does not necessarily reflect the opinion, nor it is endorsed by the OECD or the European Union.

Additional thanks also to Alexandra Tsvetkova, Alessandra Proto and other staff at the OECD Trento Centre for Local Development for hosting research visits, and the participants at the 7th meeting of the Spatial Productivity Lab of the OECD Trento Centre. Presentations to academic and policymaker audiences at the Regional Studies Association's (RSA) "Regions in Recovery Global E-Festival"; Lagos Urban Development Initiatives' "Bridge Series"; and Pitch World First's African Economy Webinar Series all provided useful reflections on content.

The authors are indebted to David Arnold for his efforts on the first iterations of this work. They are also indebted to the RSA for their efforts on the final iterations of this work to bring this book to fruition, particularly Katharina Bürger, Daniela Carl, Sally Hardy, Alex Holmes and Klara Sobekova. Helpful academic input and advice by Neil Lee and Phil Tomlinson is also gratefully acknowledged.

From the International Growth Centre (IGC), splendid graphic design that vastly improved our figures from Roelle Santa Maria, copyediting that enhanced our prose from Radhika Trivedi, and support from Victoria Delbridge and Astrid Haas are much appreciated.

Oliver would like to share a final note of thanks to Daisy Payne for her enduring earache about global value chains and willing discussions on their climate implications.

Riccardo would finally like to thank the entire ERC MASSIVE project team at the London School of Economics (LSE) whose work and internal discussions have hugely contributed to shaping the ideas and the evidence presented in this book.

The research leading to these results also received funding from the European Research Council under the European Union Horizon 2020 Programme H2020/2014–2020 [grant agreement number 639633-MASSIVE-ERC-2014-STG]. It has also received funding in-kind from the UK Foreign, Commonwealth and Development Office (FCDO) under the auspices of the International Growth Centre.

Frequent abbreviations

FDI   Foreign direct investment

FTA   Free trade agreement

GVC   Global value chain

IIPA   Inward investment promotion agency

IPA   Investment promotion agency

LCU   Local content unit

M&A   Mergers and acquisitions

MNE   Multinational enterprise

OIPA   Outward investment promotion agency

R&D   Research and development

SME   Small and medium-sized enterprise

COMPANION WEBSITE & FREE RESOURCES

Stay updated with the **latest evidence and debate** on Global Value Chains, FDI, Regional Development and Innovation by visiting the **book's companion website**. Also available to access are **free videos, presentations and learning material**. Use the QR code or visit https://blogs.lse.ac.uk/gild/books/

https:// doi.org/10.1080/2578711X.2022.2099156 © 2023 Riccardo Crescenzi and Oliver Harman

The book in a nutshell

This book combines the latest academic evidence and public policy insights on global value chains (GVCs) and foreign direct investment (FDI). It comprises a comprehensive description and explanation of why they matter for regional policy, and how subnational regions can leverage them for upgrading. Specifically, it focuses on how regions can build, embed and reshape GVCs to their local enhancement, thus bringing value to their communities and allowing them to develop.

GVCs develop the typical value chain concept—the full range of tasks that firms and workers undertake to bring a product from conception to end-use—and place it in the context of global economic integration. This includes pre-production tasks such as design and development, as well as post-production activities such as distribution and after-sales. These activities now span multiple regions, countries and continents, forming complex GVCs that account for almost 50% of global trade and comprise a significant share of global FDI, human capital and knowledge flows. Less advanced regions mostly engage in the assembly stage of the value chain—the typically lower skill and value-added section. Yet, in some cases, regions manage to shift their participation in GVCs to an increasing number of higher value-added tasks—the process of upgrading.

The book makes the case for proactive subnational public policy for the engagement of GVCs and upgrading. This approach sees regions actively engaging with GVCs rather than setting the ground and letting manna drop from heaven. Its chosen approach is three-fold.

It looks at "why": why GVCs matter and why subnational policy decision-makers should focus their attention on the opportunities offered by engagement with GVCs and upgrading. It critically reviews different streams of research and evidence in order to identify key definitions and conceptual foundations to analyse the link between GVCs, FDI and upgrading at the subnational and local levels. Secondly, it looks at "what", through new conceptualisations and critical insights on the regional drivers and impacts of global connectivity, bridging

https:// doi.org/10.1080/2578711X.2022.2099155 © 2023 Riccardo Crescenzi and Oliver Harman

macro-international and micro-firm level approaches. Thirdly it examines the critical "how": how policy decision-makers can leverage FDI and GVCs for regional benefit. The book reviews empirical evidence and available policy evaluation in order to highlight what works (and what does not) when leveraging these concepts to shape public policies, with particular reference to less-developed regions.

The book contributes to broader discussions on regional development policies including—but not limited to—Smart Specialisation. In particular, it looks at the role regional governments can play in leading the co-creation and capture of value in their economic activities. The book promotes a new GVC-sensitive approach to regional innovation strategies by offering regional decision-makers some key actionable lessons. A key lesson overall is a need to shift the paradigm in regional thinking. Instead of directing policy efforts in all regions towards new, more innovative sectors, this book suggests that attention—and resources—should be directed to value-added tasks and activities, often within existing sectors. A traditional approach to regional development has convinced regions the world over that they can innovate by developing internally, or additionally, by attracting from abroad, the oft-desired, same "flashy" information and communication technology (ICT) or biotech activities in the form of FDI. Too many regions have been convinced to look at the (very few) Silicon Valleys of the world as their models for both development and internationalisation strategies. For most, this is an error: being able to replicate their trajectories is often both unviable and, due to the unique circumstances of their creation, undesirable. Instead, this book offers policymakers the tools they need to look for development opportunities by upgrading within their existing sectors and strengths, including traditional and low-tech sectors.

1 CONNECTIVITY IS KEY

The broader lesson from the evidence on GVCs and regional innovation policy is that connectivity—actively engaging with relevant firms, investors, skills and ideas beyond national boundaries—is key. Putting up walls and retreating into domestic markets will not make regions better off. Cautious, evidence-based openness and internationalisation are important. Undertaking any protectionist measures within the connected and reliant globalised context has much higher negative fallout costs. This fallout is due to such policies impacting not only final goods but also their intermediate components. For the Organisation for Economic Co-operation and Development (OECD), these components represent, on average, half of the imports of any given country.[1]

Being open—although an essential component—is not enough. For a long time, conventional wisdom has it that economies simply need to have macroeconomic stability and openness to investment.[2] However, this neglects critical insights into specific locational differences.[3] Improvement in areas such as skills and institutional capacity is critical to ensure fruitful engagement with GVCs and local upgrading. To deliver these improvements, active public policy might be needed, which in turn requires governance input.[4] Governance input needs to be tailored to specific GVCs and the segments that governments intend to target.

2 ALL GVCS ARE DIFFERENT AND ALL REGIONS ARE DIFFERENT TO GVCS

There are significant regional disparities within countries with reference to GVC participation. In order to incorporate the relevant benefits of internationalisation, regions need to develop a value-capture strategy enabling them to benefit from their advantages in a sustained, competitive way.[5] To do so, regions must first understand the differentiated preferences and strategies of multinational enterprises (MNEs) that often act as the "lead firms" in the orchestration of GVCs. These differences are in terms of sectors, business functions, as well as the desire for knowledge and entry mode. All these complexities result in largely varied subnational geographies of GVC connectivity.[6]

3 UPGRADING AND FINE-GRAINED SPECIALISATION ARE NECESSARY

This book's diagnostic lends itself to discussion about Smart Specialisation Strategies (S3) and development policies more generally. These strategies can be twofold. First is upgrading, that is, looking at boosting current skills and capabilities within the regions' GVC-embedded industries. Second is the fostering of new regional diversification strategies within technological domains, and harnessing the potential which emerges from innovative opportunities.[7] In the GVC story, this is the process of building and embedding. Smart Specialisation echoes modern thinking about industrial policy as a "process of self-discovery".[8] However, it is necessary not just to discover and innovate, but to capture this at a regional level. Thus, Smart Specialisation is a necessary, but not sufficient, element.[9] This lack of self-discovered specialisation and upgrading is particularly evident when it comes to less developed regions. These areas suffer from an endemic absence of supportive local ecosystems—a combination of local institutions and technological, administrative, and managerial capabilities.

A critical analytic and diagnostic tool advocated in this book is to connect GVC thinking and a "Smart Specialisation" approach to regional innovation policies via GVC analysis and mapping.

Mapping regional GVCs is critical for informed decision-making on building, embedding, and reshaping GVCs. The Smart Specialisation framework also highlights the importance of this process. The diagnostic focuses on existing and evolving competitive advantages, and on the decision-making process for choosing between developing new strengths or competing based on existing ones. Learning how to work with current and future GVC actors and their potential integration is also critical, with each region being unique in its circumstances. This exercise will help regions understand how they, in particular, want to engage with GVCs. Approaches for regions on the technological frontier will differ from those in lagging regions. Depending on policy design, evidence shows that both high-income and lagging regions can grow faster or slower than average.[10] Being behind does not mean that one must remain behind. With the right policy design, internationalisation can offer new opportunities and open new trajectories, which—all things being equal—would not be available to a closed local economy.

4 BUILDING INSTITUTIONAL AND INFORMATIONAL BRIDGES MATTERS

Once regions have developed their strategy, national and regional investment promotion agencies (IPAs) have been shown to be a useful tool at the disposal of policy decision-makers for attracting the "right" kind of FDI to different types of regions, linking up with GVCs. Evidence has shown that IPAs established at both national and regional levels can enhance flows of FDI.[11] However, they must have a certain critical mass to operate effectively and, therefore, must be resourced appropriately.[12] Through the activity of dedicated organisations dealing directly with both passive (i.e., inward FDI) and active (i.e., domestic firms investing abroad) connectivity, regional decision-makers can direct FDI into value-added, task-driven activities within priority sectors. Again, these targeted tools can integrate with regional specifics.

In this context, a GVC-oriented policy paradigm would revolve around the development of institutional bridges between regional economies, their systems of innovation and the global economy. The last is a complex geography of diverse regions with their own competitive advantages and strategies. In order to profitably "bridge" (in terms of innovation and local development) different regional systems through IPAs, decision-makers should take into account two key features of GVCs.

First, outward connectivity is just as important as inward connections. Contrary to the conventional wisdom that has overstated the importance of inward FDI, outward-looking FDI will allow regional decision-makers to target related areas of the GVC, since the region itself should benefit from international investment by local domestic firms. These benefits are the knowledge connections and access to foreign markets. Regional leaders should be encouraged to make these connections or engage with national policy decision-makers to

https://doi.org/10.1080/2578711X.2022.2099155

this end. Public authorities can also contribute to the knowledge diffusion process, such as by providing advice on how to enter foreign markets.[13] A recent example was the UK Department for International Trade's 2017 insurance policy that helps UK companies invest abroad with confidence.[14]

Second, internationalisation efforts should also focus on the retention and expansion of existing locally based foreign activities. Most of the academic literature and a substantial share of national and regional policy efforts are concentrated on attracting new activities. Yet, recent evidence suggests that nurturing existing activities can be easier, cheaper and offer higher short-term returns in terms of local impacts.[15] This approach calls for a more long-term view on FDI as a key trigger for GVC participation and a means to upgrading. This long-term view is symbiotic—with both inward- and outward-FDI potentially benefiting the region—as opposed to the traditional view of FDI as a one-off transaction.

5 LEVERAGING LINKAGES

Throughout the discussion is an emphasis on linkages as critical in facilitating GVC connections to the region. To complement IPAs and bring efficient linkages between the GVC and region, it is useful to set up local content (or linkage) units (LCUs). LCUs can be part of the organisational structure of regional IPAs, and are a flexible alternative to implementing rigid laws. Instead of only written legislation, this relational-based approach, working with MNEs, can help facilitate local supply chain spillovers. The LCU can account for regional differences, and LCUs are particularly useful in lagging regions. When combined with enterprise mapping, LCUs can reduce gaps in understanding between MNEs and local agents in the host regions. While connectivity to GVCs mostly involves an elite of local firms (usually the most productive and internationalised firms acting as suppliers for MNEs, in addition to other global buyers), LCUs can contribute to enlarge this group. By doing so, they extend the benefits of GVC participation beyond the "usual suspects" and contribute to inclusive local growth.

6 THE PROACTIVE PURSUIT OF KNOWLEDGE

The final implications for regional policy decision-makers involve the proactive search for new knowledge abroad—that of learning and technology transfer from markets, firms, and workers otherwise not present in their local context. To this end, active internationalisation of firms and connecting with each other globally is the most effective. Outward-seeking activity is key to regional innovation and development, as opposed to the limitation of firms' internationalisation through the encouragement of reshoring.

Building and embedding a region into GVCs does not come without its potential drawbacks. GVCs and FDI are very integrated and enjoy strong complementarities. Policies and programmes require coordination, integration and consistency for their success.[16] However, if approaches outlined by the evidence discussed throughout this book are incorporated into regional policymakers' decisions, they will be able to help reshape their region and its interaction with the GVC. For regions, it is "not only a matter of whether to participate in the global economy, but how to do so gainfully."[17]

NOTES

1   Stephenson S and Pfister A-K (2017) Who governs global value chains? In *The Intangible Economy: How Services Shape Global Production and Consumption*. Cambridge, UK: Cambridge University Press, p. 55.

2   Williamson J (2004) *The Washington Consensus as Policy Prescription for Development*. Washington, DC: Practitioners of Development, World Bank.

3   Ponte S and Sturgeon T (2014) Explaining governance in global value chains: A modular theory-building effort. *Review of International Political Economy*, 21(1): 195–223. https://doi.org/10.1080/09 692290.2013.809596

4   Drake-Brockman J and Stephenson S (2012) Implications for 21st century trade and development of the emergence of services value chains. Paper presented at the IADB and ICTSD E-15 experts dialogue on GVCs, Geneva; Elms DK and Low P (2013) *Global Value Chains in a Changing World*. WTO/FGI/TFCTN.

5   Bailey D, Pitelis C and Tomlinson PR (2019) Strategic management and regional industrial strategy: Cross-fertilization to mutual advantage. *Regional Studies*, 1–13. https://doi.org/10.1080/00343404.20 19.1619927.

6   Crescenzi R., Pietrobelli C. & Rabellotti R (2014) Innovation drivers, value chains and the geography of multinational corporations in Europe. *Journal of Economic Geography*, 14(6): 1053-1086. doi:10.1093/jeg/lbt018

7   McCann P and Ortega-Argilés R (2015) Smart Specialization, regional growth and applications to European Union Cohesion Policy. *Regional Studies*, 49(8): 1291–1302. https://doi.org/10.1080/0034 3404.2013.799769.

8   Hausmann R and Rodrik D (2003) Economic development as self-discovery. *Journal of Development Economics*, 72(2): 603–633. https://doi.org/10.1016/S0304-3878(03)00124-X; Rodrik D, Lozachmeur J-M and Pestieau P. (2004) *Industrial Policy for the Twenty-First Century*. London: Centre for Economic Policy Research (CEPR).

9   Bailey D, Pitelis C and Tomlinson PR (2018) A place-based developmental regional industrial strategy for sustainable capture of co-created value. *Cambridge Journal of Economics*, 42(6): 1521–1542. https://doi.org/10.1093/cje/bey019.

10   Organisation for Economic Co-operation and Development (OECD) (2011) *OECD Regional Outlook 2011: Building Resilient Regions for Stronger Economies*. Paris: OECD Publ. https://www.oecd-ilibrary.org/urban-rural-and-regional-development/oecd-regional-outlook-2011_9789264120983-en.

11   Crescenzi R, Di Cataldo M and Giua M (2021) FDI inflows in Europe: Does investment promotion work? *Journal of International Economics*, 132: 103497. https://doi.org/10.1016/j.jinteco.2021.103497.

12   Melo A and Rodríguez-Clare A (2006) Productive development policies and supporting institutions in Latin America and the Caribbean. In E. Lora (ed.) *The State of State Reform in Latin America*. Palo Alto, CA: Stanford University Press.

13   Organisation for Economic Co-operation and Development (OECD) (2018) *Productivity and Jobs in a Globalised World: (How) Can All Regions Benefit?* Paris: OECD Publ.

14   Fox L (2017) Supporting overseas investment by British companies can bring vast benefits to the UK. https://www.gov.uk/government/speeches/fox-this-is-why-investors-choose-to-put-their-money-in-the-uk

15   Alvarez-Vilanova J, Crescenzi R, Di Cataldo M, Giua M and Alvarez-Vilanova J (2022) *Beyond attraction. Does investment promotion work for FDI retention and expansion?* (Mimeo). https://personal.lse.ac.uk/crescenz/InvestmentPromotion.htm

16   Crespi G, Fernández-Arias E and Stein E (2014) A world of possibilities: Internationalization for productive development. In *Rethinking Productive Development*, pp. 233–278. New York: Palgrave Macmillan.

17   Gereffi G and Fernandez-Stark K (2016) *Global Value Chain Analysis: A Primer*. Durham, NC: Duke University, p. 6. http://hdl.handle.net/10161/12488.

1. Introduction

Keywords: regions; global value chains; GVCs; foreign direct investment; FDI; tasks; connectivity

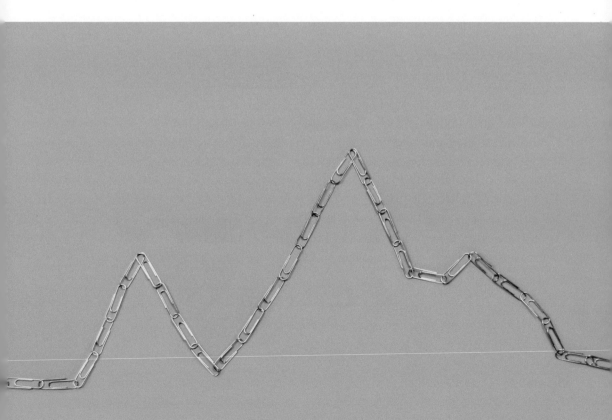

1 INTRODUCTION

This book will analyse and critically review an emerging body of evidence on the link between internationalisation, innovation and regional development. This is to provide new policy insights for regions and cities on how to build, embed and reshape global value chains (GVCs) through foreign direct investment (FDI). Therefore, it places a significant emphasis on regions and the spatial context of innovation and development policies.

The approach is to provide an evidence and policy frontier by blending published research, cutting-edge insights and successful policy cases. This blend is to highlight what is achievable for local, city and regional policy decision-makers to upgrade their regions. It builds on previous work highlighting the role that regional government has in value-added opportunities,[1] particularly its function in the identification, shaping, creation and capture of opportunities. It emphasises the importance of regions following policies that enhance their ability to co-create and capture value. More importantly, it also sheds light on the coordination of these policies with other entities, such as multinational enterprises (MNEs), which play a key role in the orchestration and governance of GVCs.[2] As prescribed elsewhere, the chapters advocate a new perspective on regional development and innovation policies which focuses on task- rather than sector-driven change.[3] The book highlights some vertical policies showing how the region can interact with the GVC. This vertical engagement is over and above conventional horizontal policies. While horizontal policies are necessary to enable an environment conducive to regional development, proactive vertical engagement can enhance the objectives of development policies from merely technological outcomes to a process of profound regional change. This method of upgrading through the value chain implies a continuous process of change with an emphasis on innovation and productivity.[4]

Our analysis begins with examining why GVCs matter. The approach entails the examination of the research to understand the emergence, evolution and geography of GVCs and introduce the concept of regional upgrading. There is an emphasis on some key actors in the GVC analysis in order to draw out some specific "what works" lessons and actionable policy. The first actor is the MNE and its role as "lead firm". The book discusses the governance role the lead firm takes up in directing the GVC, elaborating the specific types of governance and how they interact with value chain links. Subsequently, it discusses equity versus non-equity governance decisions, as one of them is more relevant to regional upgrading than the other.

After outlining the GVC governance role of MNEs, the book narrows down to another level, looking at how the MNE uses its decisions to control and coordinate activities abroad through FDI. MNEs, for example, through their FDI and broader activities, are important actors in building GVCs, and FDI often represents the first link through which regions can hook onto the chain. The GVC also shapes which regions MNEs choose as locations for their FDI. This

Regional Studies Policy Impact Books
https://doi.org/10.1080/2578711X.2022.2099162

interaction introduces a vital paradigm that links GVCs, MNEs and regions together, and the book explores this link in later chapters.

Having established and conceptualised the flow from GVC through MNEs and their FDI to the region, the book discusses the following areas: *building*, *embedding* and *reshaping* GVCs—all for regional upgrading. It identifies the gaps in which policies can impact GVCs, that is, how regions can either join or move up to more desirable sections of GVCs. *Building* and *embedding* GVCs deal with this GVC change, respectively.

In the *building GVCs through FDI* section, the focus is on locational drivers of FDI. The section first outlines the internationalisation of MNE decision-making, specifically how foreign entry modes chosen by the MNE have implications for the GVC. One entry mode of interest is greenfield investments. Such investments are a type of FDI that provide a high degree of governance control for the MNE.[5] The chapter shows that factors of both the location and the firm matter.

In the *embedding GVC through FDI* section, the focus is on impact factors. These factors are framed in two ways: first, impacts resulting from technological diffusion from MNE activities in the host economy; and second, impacts to the home economy, resulting from on- and off-shoring MNE activities. Provided there is external connectivity, the positive regional effects that the entry of an MNE can generate are foundational parts of this story. There are also wider benefits that flow back from MNE relocating activities.

In the final *reshaping GVCs through FDI section*, the focus is on public policy factors. This section looks at what regional decision-makers can do to action change upon GVCs. Decision-makers can frame these actions firstly as actions for regional leaders, both in regional institutions and international dialogue. Secondly as a diagnostic tool to better understand GVCs in a specific region, and thirdly a direct GVC sensitive regional policy to effectively enhance the link between FDI and GVCs on a local level.

These policy actions make several changes possible in practical regional policymaking. They may alter regional attractiveness to relevant sections of the GVC, and reduce barriers to entry. They may also improve understanding of the region's current place in the GVC. These actions thus sketch the region's future and provide a mechanism through which to effect this future. These are proactive steps that decision-makers can take to influence regional upgrading.

The final sections focus on a forward-looking agenda. *Looking to the future and useful tools for leveraging GVCs* focuses on what the digital and green transitions and the potential sustainable restructuring of GVCs imply for public policy. The chapter also offers some data-based tools with which to shape these changes. It closes with some concluding remarks, including broad generalised lessons, stylised due to the contextual nature of regional development.

This book is a practical step in bringing together various streams of literature and documentations of successful policy. It enhances a geographical perspective within GVCs, and links this with international business and international economics. Part of its unique contribution is the perspective of analysing the role of MNEs and FDI. It provides a valuable conceptual framework combining these streams. There is increasing discussion on the impact of regional innovation policies—and of Smart Specialisation Strategies in particular—which have increased applications in various parts of the world beyond the European Union. Some are of the opinion that such strategies have had limited success in revitalising lagging regions,[6] while others recommend getting industries and regions on new parts of GVCs to move against these regional disparities.[7] Indeed, to reverse this, it is argued that increasing the pace of which innovation spreads throughout the economy will allow regional performance to drive national productivity.[8] With GVCs at its core, this book can provide empirics and a policy framework to underpin this delivery.

The key message throughout is that connectivity and linkages are critical, especially in learning, adopting and sharing knowledge to promote upgrading as a means for sustainable development. The view should be that international knowledge, technology transfer and learning complement efforts to build region-specific innovation potential.[9] The frontier academic literature and the outline of what works in public policy provides a picture of cautious connectivity. Evidence-based internationalisation is key. However, more efforts are required to reinforce existing evidence on what works in practice both to leverage GVCs and to promote regional innovation, upgrade and develop in a sustainable manner.

NOTES

1 Foray D (2014) *Smart Specialisation: Opportunities and Challenges for Regional Innovation Policy.* Abingdon: Routledge.
2 Bailey D, Pitelis C and Tomlinson PR (2018) A place-based developmental regional industrial strategy for sustainable capture of co-created value. *Cambridge Journal of Economics*, 42(6): 1521–1542. https://doi.org/10.1093/cje/bey019.
3 Taglioni D and Winkler D (2016) *Making Global Value Chains Work for Development.* Washington, DC: World Bank. https://openknowledge.worldbank.org/handle/10986/24426
4 Organisation for Economic Co-operation and Development (OECD) (2007) *Moving Up the Value Chain: Staying Competitive in the Global Economy.* Paris: OECD Publ. https://www.oecd.org/industry/ind/stayingcompetitiveintheglobaleconomymovingupthevaluechainsynthesisreport.htm
5 Gereffi G, Humphrey J and Sturgeon T (2005) The governance of global value chains. *Review of International Political Economy*, 12(1): 78–104. https://doi.org/10.1080/09692290500049805

6   Tomlinson P, Barzotto M, Corradini C, Fai FM, Labory S and Tomlinson PR (2019) *Revitalising Lagging Regions: Smart Specialisation and Industry 4.0*. Regional Studies Policy Impact Books, 1(2): 9–12. doi:10.1080/2578711X.2019.1621095.

7   Bailey D and De Propris L (2019) 6. Industry 4.0, regional disparities and transformative industrial policy. *Regional Studies Policy Impact Books*, 1(2): 67–78. doi:10.1080/2578711X.2019.1621102.

8   Bachtler J. (2019) Towards Cohesion Policy 4.0: Structural transformation and inclusive growth. *Regional Studies Policy Impact Books*, 1(1): 1–2. doi:10.1080/2578711X.2019.1547481.

9   United Nations Conference on Trade and Development (UNCTAD) (2018) *World investment report 2018: Investment and new industrial policies* https://worldinvestmentreport.unctad.org/world-investment-report-2018/.

2. Why do GVCs matter for regions: key concepts, definitions and trends

Keywords: global value chains; GVCs; regions; foreign direct investment; FDI; multinational enterprises; MNEs; upgrading

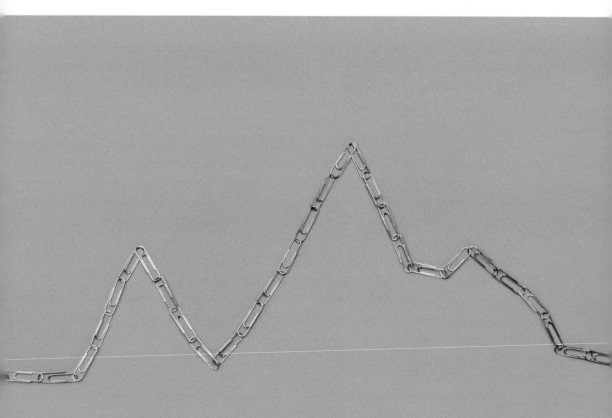

GVCs are extensively conceptualised. However, limited empirical evidence exists on the role of different actors involved in the GVC.[2] This limits the possibility of leveraging them for policy purposes. This limitation is particularly true at the subnational regional level. Hence, this section reviews the existing literature to draw new conceptual links, particularly to tie the GVC to its main governance actor: the lead firm. The lead firm is one of the building blocks underpinning GVC frameworks.[3] This section will discuss the importance of multinational enterprises (MNEs) in this context, and how policy decision-makers can leverage foreign direct investment (FDI) decisions. These decisions are the clearest way in which MNEs can "touch down" to geographical space and link up "places" through GVC connectivity. Finally, it will discuss the subnational region as the relevant unit of analysis when looking at GVCs. This regional link is central when considering strategy for placed-based policy approaches. There is increasing focus on using such policy to develop knowledge and innovation opportunities and building upon existing regional advantages and capabilities.[4] Advocates of GVCs see the potential for regions to move up the value chain, and in doing so, they reinvigorate themselves onto higher growth trajectories.[5] This book shows why GVCs can have this influence and it focuses on the parts of the value chain that policy decision-makers can affect.

> **What is the lead firm?**
>
> The lead firm is a powerful economic actor in a global value chain (GVC). They direct the chain's value-addition and distribution. This is often through governance and investment decisions such as outsourcing low-value-added activities.[1]

Regional Studies Policy Impact Books
© 2023 Riccardo Crescenzi and Oliver Harman

https://doi.org/10.1080/2578711X.2022.2099164

2.1 THE IMPORTANCE OF GLOBAL VALUE CHAINS

The concept of a GVC builds upon the idea of a "value chain":

> The value chain describes the full range of activities that firms and workers perform to bring a product from its conception to end use and beyond. This includes activities such as design, production, marketing, distribution and support to the final consumer.[6]

Value chains are complex entities with several value-added links. The base of these links or activities comprising a value chain can be in a single firm or divided across several.[7] The value chain brings together a range of activities; usually there is a heavy emphasis on the manufacturing element, but this plays only one part.[8] Value chains mark an important distinction from the "supply chain", focusing on the process of creating, capturing and sustaining value rather than just increasing supply.[9] Moreover, in the context of regional upgrading, it is important to consider where this value generation process occurs.

> A chain represents the entire input–output process that brings a product or service from initial conception to the consumer's hands.[10]

A GVC takes the typical value chain concept and places it in the context of global economic integration. This integration was made possible by conducive political and technological conditions over the past half-century. It covers activities carried out in inter-firm networks on a global scale.[11] Consider the example of a product such as flowers. Here, a simple value chain would be flowers being grown, wrapped, distributed and sold in one country by one firm. More complex value chains at the domestic level might involve an array of local and domestic actors, with distribution being carried out by a separate specialist firm. **The GVC is different: it allows the same processes to take place across many geographical spaces involving many different actors and sophisticated governance.** There could be research and development (R&D) occurring in one country attempting to produce new, rarer breeds of flowers. Those flowers could themselves be grown in another country before being packaged and branded in a third country. Another example is the iPhone. Apple develops iPhone's software and product design, but independent suppliers produce most parts of the device in different countries and different subnational regions around the world.[12] By going global, the addition of significant complexity may occur.

GVCs are not solely manufacturing focused. Not only can GVCs map out the production of a good, but also they highlight the different stages and value components required to produce a service.[13] Services are critical elements of GVCs both with regards to the services required to produce goods, and as final services targeting end-stage consumers. Within this value chain, segments at the lower value end can include basic services in information technology and

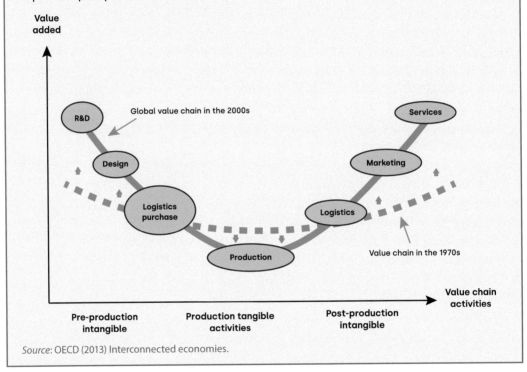
business process outsourcing. Concurrently, at the higher end, knowledge process outsourcing includes specialised market research.[14] It is thus central to note that the conceptualisation of GVCs refers both to products and services (Box 2.1).

The GVC's emergence, both as a theoretical concept and in economic reality, is relatively new. GVCs had fewer than 200 Google Scholar entries before the turn of the millennium. Between 2000 and 2013, there have been approximately 13,000 entries,[17] and around 33,000 as of 2020.

As Figure 2.1 shows, there are substantial increases in the prevalence of "global value chain" in the wider literature. Even so, there is a disconnect between the increasing importance of

Figure 2.1 The rise of global value chains: (a) Google Book Ngram Viewer (keyword term prevalence in books) [1990 – 2019]; and (b) Google trends (keyword term searched in Google) [2004 – 2021]

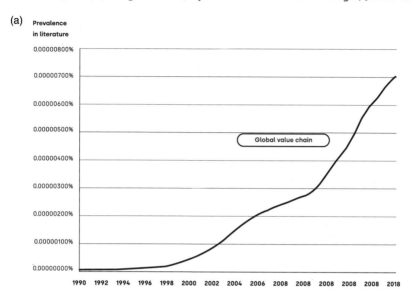

(a)

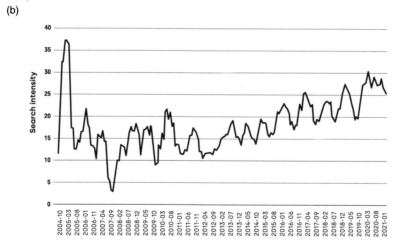

(b)

Source: Author's own elaboration of Google data

GVCs in the academic literature and the frequency of Google searches. Although the trajectory is moving upwards, the increase is not substantial. This may indicate that knowledge of and interest in GVCs had not spread to the general public.

Its newness as a concept does not take away from its importance. **GVCs account for almost 50% of global trade today.**[18] **Evidence from the period 1995–2011 highlights that all sectors, except textiles, increased their GVC participation.**[19] Even non-exporting firms will compete against imports made globally. Thus, to a large extent, participating in GVCs has become inevitable.[20] As a result of this importance, the creation of a common framework and a standard set of terms for GVCs is necessary. This creates a baseline for much of current thinking.[21] Four dimensions underpin this common framework that global value chain methodology explores:[22]

1) *Input–output* structure: the process of transforming raw materials into final products.

2) *Geographical* consideration: based on the identification of lead firms in the value chain and of the activities they orchestrate.

3) *Governance* structure: who controls the value chain.

4) *Institutional* context: where is the industry value chain embedded.

The first four dimensions saw the addition of a fifth,[23] additional analytical element:

5) *Upgrading*: the dynamic movement within the value chain by examining how producers shift between different stages.

The framework provides a comprehensive view of global industries from both the top-down and bottom-up, following the approach of some of the pioneering research on GVCs.[24] The **key concept when taking the top-down view is that of "governance"**: the role of lead firms. The **key concept when taking the bottom-up view is "upgrading"** (futher discussed and explored in 2.6 below). Lead firms are those that "govern" their global-scale supplier networks. Furthermore, identifying lead firms in each section of the value chain underpins geographical analysis.[25] They are thus of critical importance in the GVC story with its link to geographical space.

In the context of GVCs, governance is the "authority and power relationships that determine how financial, material and human resources are allocated and flow within a chain".[26] These relationships are "buyer-driven" or "producer-driven" chains.[27]

Buyer-driven chains show how important MNEs are in prescribing standards and

---

What are buyer- and producer-driven chains?

- Buyer-driven chains: these denote how global buyers use coordination to create a competent and coordinated supply base. Direct ownership or equity investment is not required. An example would be a fashion brand that designs or markets but does not make the branded products they offer
- Supplier/producer-driven chains: these denote vertically integrated supply chains. Capital- and technology-intensive production is supported by economies of scale. Here, direct FDI by MNEs is central to their evolution.[28] An example would be a car manufacturing company. The vertical integration sees lead firms make supply chain decisions for their needs with suppliers and subcontractors delivering key parts

protocols throughout their supply chain, especially in some cases with MNEs having limited production capabilities themselves. **Buyer-driven chains are more explicitly associated with "sourcing",** that is, the purchase or sale of intermediate goods. While useful for building GVCs, sourcing has less scope in embedding or reshaping GVCs. In comparison, producer-driven chains show vertical integration along all segments of the supply chain. They use technological or scale advantages from this integration. The lead firm, consequently, plays a crucial role in GVC building.

These GVCs and their buyer/producer-driven chains involve international trade flows. These trade flows can be equity or non-equity led. Equity involves networks of foreign affiliates established via FDI. These foreign affiliates are highly engaged in GVCs.[29] Non-equity involves more contractual partners and external suppliers at arm's length.[30] It is lead firms that make these strategic decisions; the scope for entering GVCs is not in the hands of countries or subnational regions. The firm's governance decisions go beyond core competencies and cost-based decisions, instead considering a complex set of factors that include productivity and sector characteristics in deciding whether to integrate. These factors help determine integration via equity or outsource via non-equity intermediate inputs.[31]

It is **these equity decisions that play a significant role in the analysis of FDI and its links with GVCs**. This is because the evidence points towards equity arrangements playing a key role in facilitating higher knowledge transfer.[33] Indeed, studies on FDI in Indonesia, China, India and Turkey show knowledge transfer occurring from foreign headquarters to acquired firms.[34] This often leads to cost savings or improvements in product quality. These equity arrangements allow inter-firm "received wisdom" to occur,[35] that is, the inter-firm nature of the connection makes technological transfer easier. This transfer extends the boundaries of the firms involved and facilitates the development of appropriate absorptive capacity. The improvement occurs in both the investing company and its equity partner.[36]

> **What is absorptive capacity?**
>
> Absorptive capacity is a firm's ability to recognise the value of new external information, particularly its ability to assimilate and apply information commercially. This capacity is critical to innovation[32]

It re-emphasises the **importance of MNE governance and FDI for knowledge transfer**. This importance is both in more traditional vertically integrated "hierarchies"[37] and alternative governance structures, such as equity joint ventures. One such example of why lead firms prefer vertical integration is the tight control over foreign production processes.[38] This control leads to new intrafirm trade and investment flows; however, the tight control can restrict upgrading. It is openness to trade and investment with well-functioning markets that are key to upgrading.[39] For every increase in openness by 1% in Organisation for Economic Co-operation and Development (OECD) nations, per capita income increases by 0.4%.[40] The fluidity allows

Figure 2.2 GVCs and MNEs

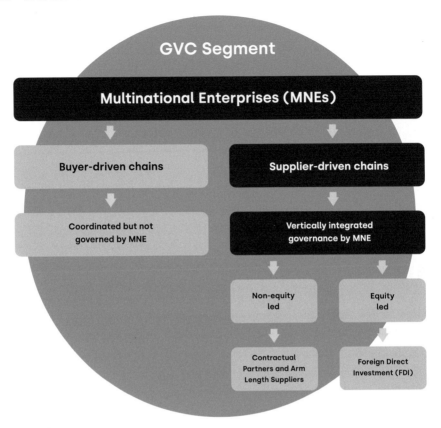

Source: Author's elaboration

the movement of resources from firms and industries which are no longer able to compete in GVCs to firms that are. This emphasises the need for reshaping policy. Figure 2.2 visualises this key area of interest.

It is important to note that with regards to regional influence, GVCs operate at different geographical scales: from local to global. They embed and "touch down" in many different parts of the world, each with specific local socio-economic and institutional dynamics.[41]

The framework uses this empirical structure to underpin its analysis.[42] The emphasis on the lead firm, that is, the MNE, and the link between its governance decisions and the geographical embedding is of prime interest. Figure 2.3 visualises the central fundamentals of this approach. It highlights how the MNE operates at the regional level, within a GVC. It also shows the simultaneous inflow–outflow nature of FDI. The same investment can be an outflow or inflow depending on the perspective of the sending and receiving region, with the firm or MNE remaining the key link. Finally, it highlights the potential two-way nature of the associated knowledge flows. The following subsections describe this visualisation in detail.

https://doi.org/10.1080/2578711X.2022.2099164

Figure 2.3   GVCs, MNEs and the regional economy

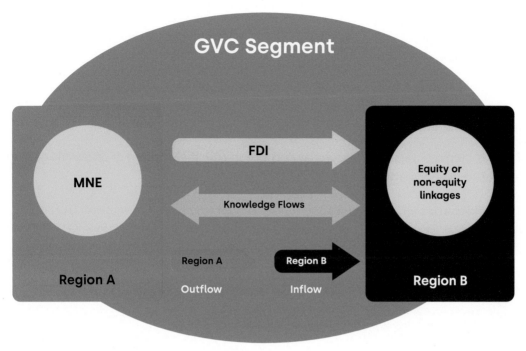

Source: Author's elaboration

2.2 THE GOVERNANCE OF GVCS AND THE ROLE OF MULTINATIONAL ENTERPRISES

Different firms interact in different ways within the GVC. The GVC, therefore, is a complex and diverse linked variety of actors. **Acknowledging and understanding the variation of the actors involved is a fundamental step** in the analysis of how to build, embed and (eventually) reshape GVCs. As discussed above, MNEs play a unique role in this context as the principal governance coordinator in GVCs. They coordinate by forming many asymmetric linkages with varied business partners. The type of these linkages varies depending on the segment of the value chain.[43]

MNEs have a critical role in the global economy. Together they account for one-third of global output and world gross domestic product (GDP), and are responsible for half of global exports.[44] Some argue that MNEs drive the recent growing fragmentation of production seen within GVCs.[45] The belief is that MNEs are also behind the global dispersion of knowledge,[46] with the reduction in the cost of moving ideas was an enabling factor in offshoring production. The dispersion of jobs followed the offshoring of production and knowledge-intensive networks. With this dispersal, knowledge diffused. It is difficult to imagine a GVC in which an MNE is not present at some stage of production.

https://doi.org/10.1080/2578711X.2022.2099164

Yet, the actual position and role of different actors such as MNEs is unclear. This under-exposure has been partially due to the limited availability of empirical evidence.[47] By looking at the governance of GVCs and the role MNEs play, **we can build further understanding of their connections and linkages**.

Historical theories of MNEs distinguish between horizontal and vertical foreign integration. Horizontal linkages are useful, but it is the vertical linkages that attempt to build, embed and reshape GVCs, which are essential for upgrading. Figure 2.4 demonstrates this.

Five basic types of value chain governance conceptualise the typology of these linkages and level of integration between the MNEs and GVCs:[49]

1) **Markets**: a simple form with markets coordinating firms and individuals who have limited interaction with one another when buying and selling products/services. An example is bicycle manufacturers with each component requiring different competencies and therefore very few firms spanning more than one segment.[50]

2) **Modular value chains**: suppliers in modular value chains producing to specific customer demands. An example is the US electronics industry with complex yet codifiable information shared between lead firms and smaller suppliers.

3) **Relational value chains**: network style requiring deeper mutual dependence. Trust and relationships in addition to spatial proximity are important. An example is the modern apparel industry in East Asia with full package supply, leading to domestically integrated supplier networks.

4) **Captive value chains**: characterised by a high degree of control by lead firms, with smaller suppliers being dependent on much larger buyers. An example is the historic apparel industry in East Asia, with textile hubs merely assembling imported inputs for lead firms.

5) **Hierarchy**: a more traditional approach where significant vertical integration means "transactions" are taking place within firm boundaries. An example is integrated firms such as Sotheby's, the British–American multinational broker of fine art and collectibles. With services ranging from scientific research (R&D), fine art storage (logistics and distribution), as well as post-sales services (sales), much of its highly complex transactions and tasks rely heavily on tacit—or implicit—sharing of knowledge.

MNEs fit in around **relational value chains, captive value chains, and hierarchy**. These need, respectively, more significant degrees of coordination and power variation.[51] MNEs have firm-specific advantages that they may want to internalise. To do so, some governance structures are more effective than others. The effectiveness depends on the motives driving internalisation decisions. For instance, substantial vertical integration (hierarchical vertically integrated value chains) facilitates understanding that only proximity (co-location) can bring in other governance structures.[52]

    https://doi.org/10.1080/2578711X.2022.2099164

Figure 2.4   Horizontal and vertical MNE linkages

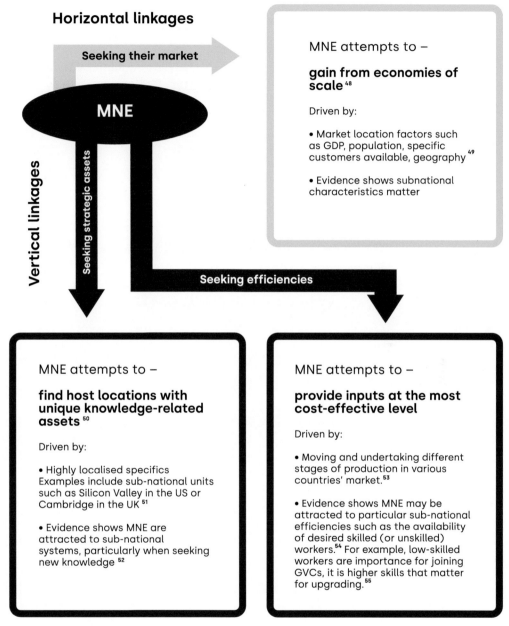

Sources: Authors' own elaboration.[48]

By including networks, the typology helps to show why, in today's global economy, MNEs seem to function as systems within the international production systems of GVCs.[53] This power in different types of governance ties back with the previously mentioned supplier/producer-driven chains, especially the role of FDI in coordinating their evolution.

There is a **shift in focus from horizontal towards more vertical MNE activities in GVCs**.[54] With this, the idea gaining promise is that trade and investment have become complements instead of substitutes. While often described as "two sides of the same coin",[55] the intertwining of trade and investment is in a more complex manner within GVCs.[56] However, currently, the evidence base cannot provide enough detail (particularly in geographical terms) to sufficiently analyse the trade–investment interaction within GVCs.[57] The policy framework will, therefore, be on FDI and global investment flows.

2.3 THE SIGNIFICANCE OF FOREIGN DIRECT INVESTMENT FOR GVCS AND THEIR LOCALISATION

According to the standard understanding of MNE investment motives, MNEs invest abroad if they have one (or more) of three types of advantages. This is the ownership, location and internalisation (OLI) framework.[58] This foundation of global investment flows is helpful in developing an initial understanding of investment flows in order to build (as a first approximation and in the waiting for more academic work on investment motives) a GVC layer upon it.

- An **ownership advantage** is something MNEs "**possess**". It provides them with an advantage abroad to overcome their unfamiliarity with local conditions. Examples are often present in the realm of technology and knowledge.

- A **location advantage** is something MNEs **"desire"** that ties them to a specific location. In other words, it is an advantage specific to a particular location. Examples are potential inputs such as the knowledge base and high human capital, or a demand factor such as the size of the potential market.

- An **internalisation advantage** is something MNEs **"acquire"**. It ties activities integrating them vertically to the company's internal organisation, as opposed to externally contracting them. This advantage is most important when thinking of an MNE's equity versus non-equity investment decisions.

However, when analysing MNEs in the context of GVCs, we need to further develop thinking on MNE investment motives and decisions, given that these are now part of a much wider web of international input–output linkages wherein the ultimate objective is the generation and capture of added value.

It is these MNE decisions with their associated linkages and governance that the lead firm can use to expand its value chain operations. **MNEs are well placed to take a risk and seek out locational advantages.** They are the driving force behind most variants of firm governance in GVCs. MNEs achieve this through their investment, outsourcing and offshoring activities.[59]

Domestically, this expansion can occur through the headquarters of the MNE, which is often already a multi-location, multi-establishment domestic firm. The headquarters and/or other domestic establishments develop supply chain networks and linkages with other large MNEs operating in their home market, other large purely domestic firms and, in some cases, SMEs. It is this provision of intermediate inputs or service-based tasks that draws a wider circle of selected suppliers into GVCs.[60]

The participation of domestic non-MNEs into GVCs is highly selective and involves a limited number of "frontier firms" that act as first-tier suppliers to key GVC hubs/MNEs.[61] This first tier of advanced suppliers is then linked to a diverse constellation of second- and third-tier suppliers. **The extent, depth and nature of this local constellation of "indirectly GVC-linked" firms is highly dependent on industry characteristics** (e.g., in the automotive sector the structure of suppliers is different from that of the apparel and footwear sectors) **and supply chain type** (buyer versus producer driven). When abroad, this expansion can be undertaken by expanding equity-based FDI or non-equity outsourcing. In order to guide and enhance regional dynamics, there is a need to determine and support key "vehicles" that link to GVCs firms that are active in the domestic local economy. **FDI is one of these vehicles,**[62] as FDI acts as a catalyst for GVC integration through foreign capital and technical knowhow. Its utilisation is particularly prevalent for upgrading in lagging regions with, for example, scarce capital. Thus, GVC activity and FDI inflows go hand in hand, often accompanying upgrading.[63] In the specific cases of China and some Latin American countries—namely Mexico—studies show that international trade and FDI were central to industrial upgrading.[64]

FDI, when viewed from the firms' perspective, implies the circulation of capital and information. The exchange involves physical capital, human capital and knowledge across the MNE corporate network, including central and regional headquarters and subsidiaries of different roles and levels in the functional hierarchy. However, it is also crucial to consider geography: when placed in a regional perspective, FDI can occur as either an inflow or an outflow to the region. For the former, when an MNE starts a new activity in a foreign region that hosts it, and for the latter, through the offshoring of activities by a local company towards a foreign region. Both have different (perceived or actual) local impacts that need to be considered individually.

With this vehicle, MNEs can build, embed and reshape GVCs through the FDI they establish. It is primarily through FDI that regions can benefit from GVCs. Therefore, FDI as a key MNE tool needs examination.

FDI is one of the institutional forms that MNEs use to control and coordinate activities abroad.[65] The development of GVCs has triggered a shift of motivations for entering foreign markets,[66] with increased fragmentation of strategic MNE activity altering investment decisions. The slight refining of FDI motivations illustrates that location choice can also depend on two other elements: first, on value chain segment; and second, on the governance modality used by the MNE when participating in a host economy.[67]

The relationship between FDI and building GVCs is that FDI represents the first link by which many regions can hook onto the chain. FDI represents the interaction between the globally acting, footloose MNE and the spatially fixed region.[68] It also represents access. Its description is one of **the catalysts for GVC integration**.[69] The relationship between FDI and embedding GVCs is through FDI's ability to facilitate the transfer of capability.[70] Therefore, some discussion must take place within MNEs on which key activities and capabilities they should keep at the headquarters and which they should relocate. Those chosen to relocate attempt to harness new specific regional endowments. There is, however, a particular set of conditions that make some decision-making more natural than others.[71] These environments may lead to more innovation-prone interactions and institutions occurring in some localities over others. Since MNEs delocalise different functions, different levels of local embeddedness are required.[72] Depending on the part of the value chain that will be relocated, the locational preferences of MNEs will differ.[73] In other words, **the GVC shapes the relationship between FDI and regions**.

Figure 2.5 represents our focus by taking one element of the larger GVC (the lead firm), one element of the lead firm (its FDI flows) and how this relationship interacts with the region.

Figure 2.5   How FDI links global values chains (GVCs) and regions

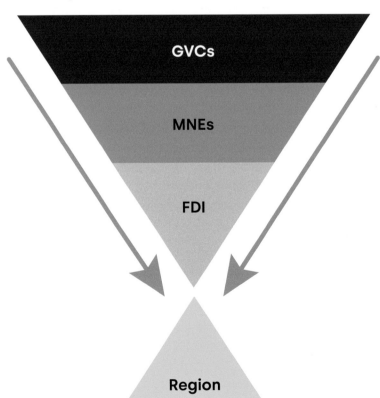

Source: Author's elaboration

There is also a link between GVC participation and FDI, and the GVC participation index outlines the extent of this link. FDI therefore influences a country's GVC participation through the nature of its investments and the links it generates with local suppliers and other firms in the regional ecosystem. Until 2012, GVCs had shown two decades of growth.[78] However, since then, GVC participation has decreased despite these large flows. This reduction was across all regions, both developed and developing.[79] This GVC slowdown correlates with a simultaneously occurring slowdown in FDI, reaffirming the **strong impact FDI has on global trade patterns**.

Likewise, there is a strong impact on economic fundamentals. Estimations show a 1% increase in GVC participation boosts income levels by more than 1%—about twice as much as conventional trade.[80] Moreover, since 1970, those areas with high GVC participation generally experienced faster growth rates for labour productivity than others.[81] This is even more prominent in countries with lower income, where there is a strong potential benefit to catching up with leaders of productivity through GVC participation. Poor countries and poor regions grew faster than the average.[82] While this productivity may not always lead to job growth,[83] it should ultimately translate into higher real wages. It is therefore **even more critical that regional leaders grasp how best to benefit from FDI flows in and out of their regions**.

2.4 THE ROLE OF SUBNATIONAL REGIONS IN GVC AND FDI

For the purpose of this discussion, two relevant boundaries identify the region as a sub-national unit of space. Either institutional/administrative (e.g., *Landers* in Germany or *Regioni* in Italy) or economically functional boundaries (e.g., travel-to-work areas in the UK or metropolitan statistical areas in the United States), although these boundaries overlap sometimes. The region is a critical unit when drawing links with the GVC, particularly in bridging the macro-national level and micro-firm perspectives. **GVCs "touch down" or are "built" in many different parts of the world and are embedded within local economic, social, and institutional dynamics.**[84] Furthermore, GVCs and wider global megatrends will increase the importance of place-based policy.[85] Yet they are rarely discussed, despite their effects being far from uniform within nations.[86] These local, placed-based conditions

Figure 2.6   Maps of FDI (a) inflow and (b) outflow by region, 2003–17

(a) *FDI Inflow*

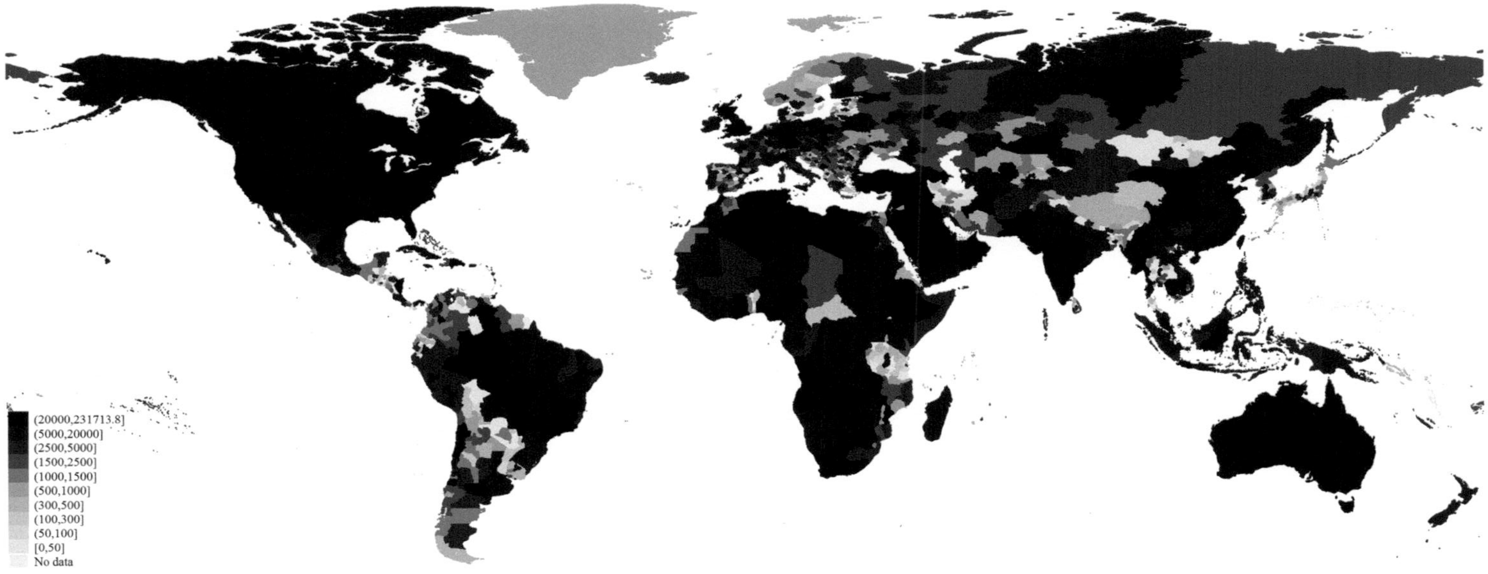

[20000,231713.8]
[5000,20000]
(2500,5000]
(1500,2500]
(1000,1500]
(500,1000]
(300,500]
(100,300]
(50,100]
[0,50]
No data

                                    https://doi.org/10.1080/2578711X.2022.2099164

Figure 2.6 (Continued)

(b) *FDI Outflow*

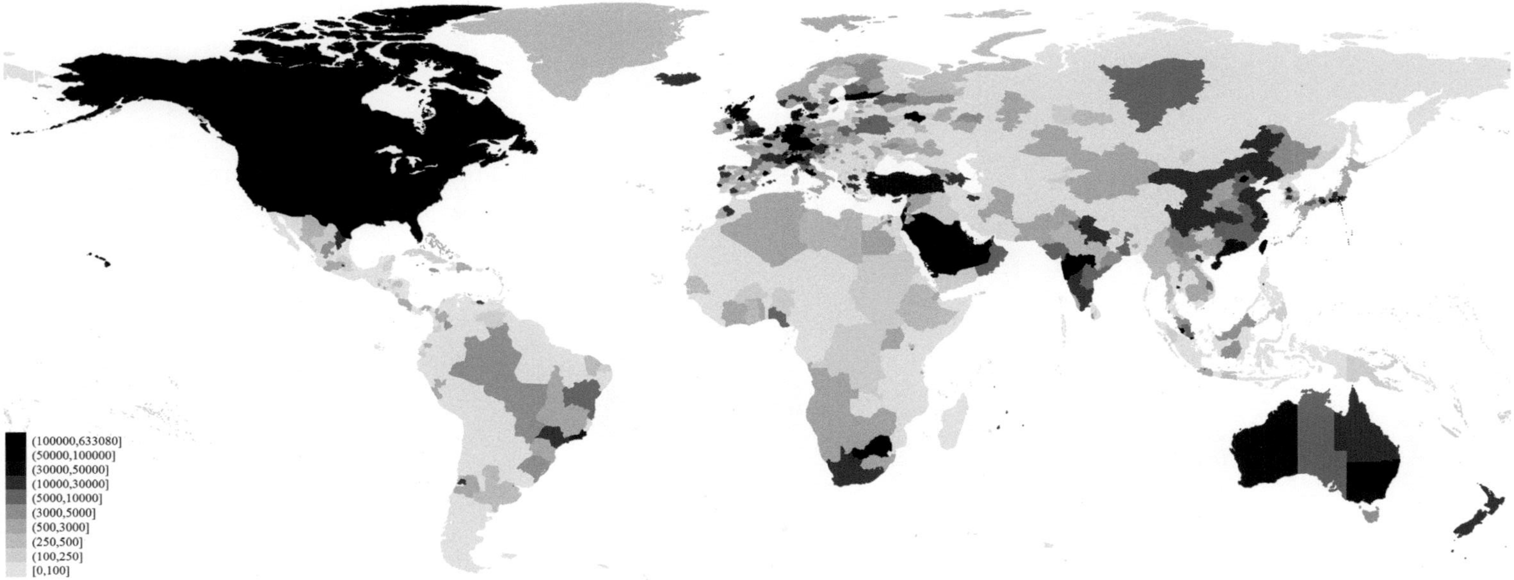

	[100000,633080]
	[50000,100000]
	[30000,50000]
	[10000,30000]
	[5000,10000]
	[3000,5000]
	[500,3000]
	[250,500]
	[100,250]
	[0,100]

Source: Authors' elaborations on Fdi Markets data by *The Financial Times*

make a significant contribution to how effective insertion into the GVC may be—it differs highly both between and within countries. Recent regional policy initiatives (such as Smart Specialisation Strategy—S3) now include an approach accounting for space, and are linked with value creation and capture.[87] This approach builds upon the notion that regions can build spatial competitive advantages and generate new specialisms. Finding high(er) value niches in a range of global industries rather than a race-to-the-bottom-style competition on commodity prices or cheap labour is increasingly adopted as the upgrading approach.[88] Generation occurs through the "discovery of new domains of opportunity and local concentration and agglomeration of resources and competencies in these domains",[89] that is, the identification and leveraging of local, fine-grained specialisms.

Since there is a focus on FDI, the locational factors of the flows matter. This focus is on both where the outflow originates from, for example, the MNE headquarters (HQ), and on where the inflow reaches, for example, building a foreign, ground-up greenfield investment. Thus, regions adopt a different perspective of FDI to firms. It is this conceptual link with the region and the insights it provides that is followed throughout this analysis. **Actionable change is much clearer by influencing global investment decisions in this manner.** FDI is also much easier to measure and track in comparison with GVCs in their entirety and complexity. With GVCs, it can be difficult to show clear trends given available data and methods, particularly with regards to specific, intangible resources.[90]

Notably, empirics show there are two contrasting stories with the evolving FDI picture, one of inflows and one of outflows. Inflows as a world total have grown from under US$1000 billion in 2005 to US$1430 billion in 2018.[91] This rise is primarily driven by developing countries, which now represent half of all FDI inflows. For developing countries and regions, foreign capital is critical for GVC integration.[92] However, outflows are still dominated by developed economies. To a significant extent, the competition to attract FDI has intensified in parallel with this surge in recent decades.[93] We can trace these flows, their home and host regions, and the associated patterns of dispersion and concentration. The mapping of investment flows is shown in Figure 2.6, and two key things are clear. First, the significant variation in investment flows at the subnational level is seen in every continent, and especially in countries such as Argentina, Mexico, Tanzania, Spain and Japan. Second, there is a stark contrast between the concentration of FDI inflows and outflows in areas such as Europe and the United States, as opposed to FDI in South America and Sub-Saharan Africa.

It is clear subnational units matter. Therefore, to develop concrete local policies, discussion must go beyond that of the national unit. This change is driven by two parts: first, the need to examine theoretically the different levels of geography often seen within MNE operations better; and second, due to the different characteristics of value chain stages having different effects on location decisions.[94] The traditional location drivers described above that the MNE might desire, such as market size, play a different role. Instead, softer locational drivers that might facilitate MNE

https://doi.org/10.1080/2578711X.2022.2099164

investment, such as institutional capacity, are important.[95] These softer drivers might be the existence of various institutional supports or innovation system characteristics. These drivers are particularly necessary for sophisticated GVC functions such as R&D or design business services.[96]

Cluster policy brings further parallels of subnational links. Evidence shows that when a cluster becomes part of a value chain, the impact can be transformative.[97] Following this intuition, sections of this book that look at building and embedding GVCs will show how linking a region with a GVC can be beneficial, although GVC integration by region has marked differences.[98]

Placing the thinking behind regional decision-making in line with this conceptual outline will enable the following "what works" interventions to be more effective. Without drawing the link from the GVC to the MNE and then to the regional setting via FDI, these otherwise transnational actors would not be able to tie into an influenceable area.

GVC integration varies substantially both between and within countries. **Generally, most countries lie between 15% and 25% integration with GVCs**[99]—these figures representing, as a share of total trade, how much crosses at least two borders before the end consumer.[100] However, the shares across regions within a country can often fluctuate by a further 10 percentage points each way. This integration story has remained relatively stable over time, with limited convergence. While the top quarter of regions harbours more than 30% of value-added from economic activities within the GVC, the estimate is closer to 11% for the bottom quarter.[101]

These global FDI figures and MNE expansion are useful in providing a more comprehensive global picture. However, at the regional level, there are specific disparities that are useful to highlight. Intra-country FDI can vary considerably in terms of stock and yearly change.[102] Inflows and outflows can increase at different rates. This occurs, for example, in the subnational units of Wschodni and Północno-Zachodni in Poland. Further still, inflows and outflows may move in opposite directions, as seen in the subnational units of Mecklenburg-Wester Pomerania and Baden-Wurttemberg in Germany. **A successful FDI strategy at the national level may mean very different things for regions at a subnational level.** These connectivity disparities and differing trajectories are not unique to Europe: regional concentration and stock of FDI shows similar in-country variance in both Russia and Brazil, too.[103]

The above indicates **clear evidence and potential policy implications for why GVCs are important for regions**, and why they deserve attention and active policy engagement. The exploration of the policy actions alluded to occurs hereafter. The discussion focuses on how the lack of GVC participation and convergence can reverse, and how regional decision-makers can use global investment flows for their benefit, thus upgrading through building, embedding and reshaping GVCs. However, before progressing, policy decision-makers need to ensure that they have the right perspective.

2.5 CHANGING THE PERSPECTIVE—OLD PARADIGM VERSUS NEW PARADIGM

MNEs have driven the increasing fragmentation of the global economic system over the past few decades. **They have changed its economic makeup.** Today, more than half of the world's manufactured imports are intermediate goods. They are also job creators, with about two-thirds of all production-generated jobs accruing from indirect (or intermediate good) exporters.[105] These goods may be primary goods, semi-finished products, or parts and

> **What is an intermediate good and service?**
>
> An intermediate good is a product used as an input or component in the production of a final product. They are typically sold between industries for resale and are therefore semi-finished. Steel panels for chassis is a good example for the car industry.
>
> An intermediate service similarly services as an input into the production of other goods or services. Such services critically affect an economy's competitiveness.[104] Storage or financing for the car industry are good examples

components. Furthermore, over 70% of world services imports are intermediate services.[106] Intermediate goods and services are a crucial part of global production and GVCs. Instead of sectors themselves, it seems to be the way goods are produced, the knowledge intensity in this process and the resultant quality that may be defining matters.[107]

Before moving further, it is worth noting that the evidence points towards a new perspective of thinking. The integrated nature of the global economy means we can **no longer look at regional production through a sector-driven lens**. That is, policy decision-makers should move away from focusing on how to shift from low- or high-value sectors focusing on the final good. Rather, the production of goods in the same sector can occur with very different technologically driven tasks. This occurs with either backward technology that has limited skill intensity in one country, or instead, modern, skill-intensive technology in another country.[108] **It is the tasks that matter.** It is through tasks that subnational units can compete and build micro-comparative advantages in specific production stages. This is as opposed to a more difficult-to-attain final goods advantage. Tasks allow for fine-grained specialisms,[109] building on local strengths to form niche sectors, exploiting locational advantages and harnessing local skills.[110]

Focusing on certain parts or tasks favours the diffusion of technology—an important driver of innovation. It also helps with access to capital. As a result, productivity and income growth increase. For example, firms in Ethiopia that participate in GVCs are 50% as productive as those participating in standard trade.[111] This is the case in many developing countries, particularly those moving from commodity exporting to import-to-export light manufacturing, such as in Bangladesh, Cambodia and Viet Nam's garment trade. Evidence shows that three years after joining a manufacturing GVC, a country is typically 20% richer per capita.[112] Yet, to stay relevant, these tasks must go through a process of dynamic specialisation progressing to more

https://doi.org/10.1080/2578711X.2022.2099164

sophisticated activities. Examples of this specialisation based on locational advantages might include focusing on logistics and distribution tasks for regions with ports. Similarly, R&D-related activities are well placed in areas where local human capital skills mimic this progression.

The fragmentation of production associated with GVCs has now provided cross-country firms with the opportunity to engage in global trade. Firms lack the burden of the necessity to develop the full range of vertical capabilities across the value chain themselves.[113] Therefore, when viewing the GVC and its potential benefits, **we should have a task-driven lens. This lens looks at low- or high-value activities *within* sectors, focusing on the intermediate good.**[114]

Critically, we must consider two other elements:

- Linking to the GVC.

- Moving up the GVC.

Linking with the GVC is the process of **building** the connection—the region's "locational" factors. Moving up the GVC is the process of **embedding** the connection—and enhancing the "impact" upon the region.[115] **GVCs have denationalised comparative advantage**, making locational factors more fundamental. A firm's location choices are, after all, task specific.[116] Similarly, they represent a sure opportunity for upgrading regional skills and competitive offering, which can result in dynamic improvements in regional innovative networks.

The paradigm must change from thinking only of tangible production to considering other intangible inputs into the GVC. These include, but are not limited to, R&D, design, marketing, branding and distribution. Figure 2.7 highlights this with the change in perspective of industry

Figure 2.7   Old versus new paradigm in regional development

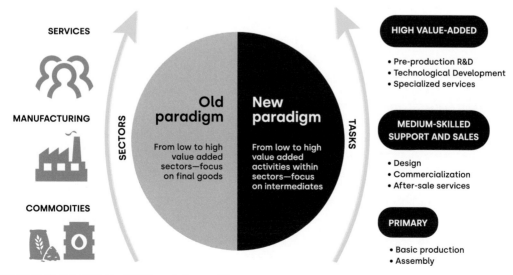

Source: Taglioni and Winkler (2016), see Reference 75

https://doi.org/10.1080/2578711X.2022.2099164

development. The old paradigm on the left shows the previously followed development trajectory—that of moving from commodities to manufacturing and finally services.

However, the shift in developing thinking onto the new paradigm means upgrading into high-value segments instead. These segments are of the industries in which regions have already established expertise. Figure 2.7 indicates that these activities are within sectors, although there will be some transferability across sectors depending on the required skills. **This new perspective in a GVC-oriented world results in an industrial policy based on specialisation in specific functions**. It has important implications for our understanding of regional development and innovation.

2.6 REGIONAL UPGRADING

The **concept of upgrading** and its process can be summarised as,

> firms, countries, or regions moving to higher value activities in GVCs in order to increase the benefits (e.g. security, profits, value-added, capabilities) from participating in global production.[117]

Arguably, because **upgrading drives non-patenting innovation, developing regions and countries can leverage upgrading as a development strategy.** It sees a region innovate, although it removes the tie to product innovation and patentable technologies. By participating in more profitable tasks that are more sophisticated or complex in nature, regions can add more value and progressively catch up with the technological frontier at their own pace and through their own pathway.

Regional policy decision-makers have numerous potential upgrading successes that change the traditional approach. This change moves away from the narrow focus on productivity and product innovation measured by patents and other strict technological performance indicators. Instead, knowledge-based capital is harnessed in other ways.

Upgrading occurs in many different forms.

Horizontal upgrading accounts for the first type of upgrading and **refers to the development of a new GVC product or industry in a region that is related to an existing GVC**. For example, the manufacturing of mobile phones may follow from existing production of laptops.

Horizontal upgrading includes three frameworks for upgrading. **Chain or inter-sectoral upgrading**[118] refers to firms moving into new but related industries. **Entry into the supply chain upgrading**[119] specifies the inaugural participation of firms in a local, regional, or global value chain. In **end market upgrading,** firms move into more sophisticated markets which require new or more demanding standards.[120]

https://doi.org/10.1080/2578711X.2022.2099164

The second type of upgrading is **vertical upgrading**, which **offers a new function for the manufacturers**; for example, R&D, or marketing, logistics, headquarters management, and perhaps production in an existing value chain. If horizontal upgrading describes a movement from laptop production to mobile phone manufacturing, vertical upgrading describes the movement from mobile phone production to mobile phone design.

Four frameworks[121] fit within vertical upgrading. **Process upgrading** refers to firms and workers transforming inputs to outputs more efficiently. **Product upgrading** refers to firms and workers moving into more sophisticated product lines. In **functional upgrading,** firms and workers increase the skill content of tasks. Meanwhile, in **backward linkages upgrading,** local firms become active in an industry supplying goods and services to an MNE in a foreign country already engaged in an existing value chain. There is an inherent trade-off, depending on which upgrading route is sought. While evidence at the national scale shows that horizontal upgrading is less difficult to achieve than vertical upgrading, the variation from industry to industry and country to country is substantial.

The types of linkages and the direction of upgrading is important to consider. With respect to vertical linkages, regions can upgrade through forward and backward linkages. Forward linkages, also known as downstream linkages, refer to upgrading with firms further along the value chain; that is, firms closer to final goods or eventual export. Backward linkages, also known as upstream linkages, refer to linkages closer to suppliers or initial goods, or creation of services. Upgrading does not necessarily mean moving upstream or downstream. Rather, it is the process of climbing up the value chain. This co-directionality is detailed further in the below case study.

Case study 1: Non-patent regional upgrading and innovation in Torreón, Mexico[122]

A case study of successful upgrading at the regional level is Torreón, Mexico. Initially, apparel suppliers in the area were only providing value in the assembly stage of the blue jeans industry there. However, between 1993 and 2000 through upgrading activities, they were able to work in higher value-added segments. Such upgrading was two-fold. First, product upgrading entailed new distinct washes and finishes. Second, inter-sectoral upgrading developed expertise in distribution. They were becoming embedded within the value chain.

In 2004, facing a US export demand shift to China, Torreón was forced to reinvent itself further and again climb up the value chain. This time it had to move from a region predominantly providing tangible material inputs to pre- and post-production intangible inputs. This upgrading occurred through the development of local brands and the establishment of a local design centre. Both created new links with other GVCs, added higher value and allowed the subnational unit to reshape GVC policy

---

With this paradigm shift, **upgrading offers an alternative or complementary regional development pathway** - one that is centred on tasks, compared to the traditional one centred on structural change and changing sectoral make up (Figure 2.7). The new paradigm attempts to move local economic activity onto more complicated tasks in which a region or city has an existing advantage. Understanding and finding this advantage explains the criticality of focusing on the subnational, as each region will have a specific trajectory and specific comparative advantage to leverage for development. Well-functioning regions leveraging micro specialisms translate into national socio-economic gain.

NOTES

1 Khattak A and Stringer C (2016) The role of suppliers in the greening of GVCs: Evidence from the Sri Lankan apparel industry. In MM Erdogdu, T Arum and IH Ahmad (eds.), *Handbook of Research on Green Economic Development Initiatives and Strategies*, pp. 539–559. Hershey, PA: IGI Global. http://dx.doi.org/10.4018/978-1-5225-0440-5.ch023

2 Cadestin C, De Backer K, Desnoyers-James I, Miroudot S, Ye M and Rigo D (2018) Multinational enterprises and global value chains: New insights on the trade–investment nexus. *OECD Science, Technology and Industry Working Papers* 2018(5): 1–36. https://doi.org/10.1787/194ddb63-en.

3 Gereffi G (2018) The emergence of global value chains: Ideas, institutions and research communities. In *Global Value Chains and Development: Redefining the Contours of 21st Century Capitalism*. Cambridge: Cambridge University Press for Foundations of the Global Value Chain Framework. doi:10.1017/9781108559423.002.

4 Barca F, McCann P and Rodríguez-Pose A (2012) The case for regional development intervention: Place-based versus place-neutral approaches. *Journal of Regional Science* 52(1): 134–152. https://doi.org/10.1111/j.1467-9787.2011.00756.x

5 Bailey D, Pitelis C and Tomlinson PR (2018) A place-based developmental regional industrial strategy for sustainable capture of co-created value. *Cambridge Journal of Economics* 42(6): 1521–1542. https://doi.org/10.1093/cje/bey019

6 Gereffi G, Fernandez-Stark K and Psilos P (2011) *Skills for Upgrading: Workforce Development and Global Value Chains in Developing Countries*. Duke University, Center on Globalization, Governance and Competitiveness (Duke CGGC), RTI International. https://gvcc.duke.edu/wp-content/uploads/Skills-for-Upgrading-Workforce-Development-and-GVC-in-Developing-Countries_FullBook-3.pdf

7 Frederick S (2016) *GVCs Concepts & Tools*. Duke University. https://globalvaluechains.org/concept-tools.

8 Gereffi G (1999) A commodity chains framework for analyzing global industries. *Institute of Development Studies* 8(12): 1–9.

9 Gereffi (2018), see Reference 3.

10 Gereffi et al. (2011), see Reference 6.

11 Gereffi et al. (2011), see Reference 6.

12 Xing Y (2011) How the iPhone widens the US trade deficit with China. *VoxEU*.

13 Gereffi G (2001) Beyond the producer-driven/buyer-driven dichotomy: The evolution of global value chains in the internet era. *IDS Bulletin*, 32(3): 30–40; Sturgeon TJ (2001) How do we define value chains and production networks? *IDS Bulletin*, 32(3): 9–18.

14 Fernandez-Stark K, Bamber P and Gereffi G (2011) The offshore services value chain: Upgrading trajectories in developing countries. *International Journal of Technological Learning, Innovation and Development* 4(1–3): 206–234. https://hdl.handle.net/10161/16489

15 Organisation for Economic Co-operation and Development (OECD) (2013) *Interconnected Economies*. OECD Publ.

16 Baldwin R and Ito T (2021) The smile curve: Evolving sources of value added in manufacturing. *Canadian Journal of Economics/Revue canadienne d'économique* 54(4): 1842–1880.

17 World Trade Organization (WTO) (2014) *World Trade Report: Trade and Development: Recent Trends and the Role of the WTO*. Geneva: WTO.

18 World Bank (2020) *World Development Report 2020: Trading for Development in the Age of Global Value Chains*. Washington, DC: World Bank.

19 World Bank (2020), see Reference 18.

20 Gereffi G and Luo X (2015) Risks and opportunities of participation in global value chains. *Journal of Banking and Financial Economics* 2(4): 51–63.

21 Gereffi (2018), chs 2–4; see Reference 3.

22 As outlined in Gereffi G and Fernandez-Stark K (2016) *Global Value Chain Analysis: A Primer*. Duke University. http://hdl.handle.net/10161/12488.

23 Gereffi G (1999) International trade and industrial upgrading in the apparel commodity chain. *Journal of International Economics*, 48(1): 37–70; Humphrey J and Schmitz H (2002) How does insertion in global value chains affect upgrading in industrial clusters? *Regional Studies*, 36(9): 1017–1027. https://doi.org/10.1080/0034340022000022198

24 Gereffi G (2010) The global economy: Organization, governance, and development. In N Smelser and R Swedberg (eds.), *The Handbook of Economic Sociology*, pp. 160–182. Princeton, NJ: Princeton University Press.

25 Gereffi et al. (2011), see Reference 6.

26 Gereffi G (1994) The organization of buyer-driven global commodity chains: How US retailers shape overseas production networks. In G Gereffi and M Korzeniewicz (eds.), *Commodity Chains and Global Capitalism*, pp. 95–95. Westport, CN: Praeger.

27 Gereffi G (1994), see Reference 26.

28 Gereffi (2001), see Reference 13.

29 Altomonte C, Di Mauro F, Ottaviano G, Rungi A and Vicard V (2012) Global value chains during the great trade collapse: A bullwhip effect in firms. In S Beugelsdijk, S Brakman, H van Ees and H Garretsen (eds.), *International Economy: Firm Heterogeneity Meets International Business*, pp. 277–308. MIT Press.

30 Taglioni D and Winkler D (2014) Making global value chains work for development. *World Bank – Economic Premise* 143: 1–10. https://openknowledge.worldbank.org/handle/10986/24426

31 Antras P and Helpman E (2004) Global sourcing. *Journal of Political Economy*, 112(3): 552–580.

32 Cohen WM and Levinthal DA (1990) Absorptive capacity: A new perspective on learning and innovation. *Administrative Science Quarterly*, 35(1): 128–152.

33 Mowery DC, Oxley JE and Silverman BS (1996) Strategic alliances and interfirm knowledge transfer. *Strategic Management Journal*, 17(S2): 77–91.

34 Javorcik B (2019) *Eight Things Development Professionals Should Know about Foreign Direct Investment*. PEDL Synthesis Series, Private Enterprise Development in Low-Income Countries. Washington, DC: Center for Economic and Policy Research.

35 Kogut B (1988) Joint ventures: Theoretical and empirical perspectives. *Strategic Management Journal*, 9(4): 319–332.

36 Cohen and Levinthal (1990), see Reference 32.

37 Oxley JE (1997) Appropriability hazards and governance in strategic alliances: A transaction cost approach. *Journal of Law, Economics, and Organization*, 13(2): 387–409.

38 World Bank (2020), see Reference 18.

39 OECD (2007) *Moving Up the Value Chain: Staying Competitive in the Global Economy*. Paris: OECD Publ.

40 OECD (2007), see Reference 39

41 Gereffi et al. (2011), see Reference 6.

42 Gereffi G (1995) Global production systems and Third World development. In B Stallings (ed.), *Global Change, Regional Response: The New International Context of Development*. Cambridge: Cambridge University Press; Gereffi G, Humphrey J and Sturgeon T (2005) The governance of global value chains. *Review of International Political Economy*, 12(1): 78–104.

43 Ponte S and Sturgeon T (2014) Explaining governance in global value chains: A modular theory-building effort. *Review of International Political Economy*, 21(1): 195–223. https://doi.org/10.1080/09692290.2013.809596

44 Cadestin et al. (2018), see Reference 2.

45 Cadestin et al. (2018), see Reference 2.

46 Baldwin R (2016) *The Great Convergence: Information Technology and the New Globalisation*. Cambridge, MA: Harvard University Press.

47 Cadestin et al. (2018), see Reference 2.

48 [a]Author's elaboration based on Cadestin et al. (2018), see Reference 2.
[b]For different variables, see Loree DW and Guisinger SE (1995) Policy and non-policy determinants of US equity foreign direct investment. *Journal of International Business Studies*, 26(2): 281–299; Flores RG and Aguilera RV (2007) Globalization and location choice: An analysis of US multinational firms in 1980 and 2000. *Journal of International Business Studies*, 38(7): 1187–1210; Beugelsdijk S and Mudambi R (2014) MNEs as border-crossing multi-location enterprises: The role of discontinuities in geographic space. In J Cantwell (ed.), *Location of International Business Activities*, pp. 8–34. Basingstoke: Palgrave Macmillan; Crescenzi R (2021) Changes in economic geography theory and the dynamics of technological change. In MM Fischer and P Nijkamp (eds.), *Handbook of Regional Science*, pp. 1307–1324. Berlin: Springer.

[c]Crescenzi et al. (2014), see Reference 73.

[d]Cantwell J and Piscitello L (1999) The emergence of corporate international networks for the accumulation of dispersed technological competences. *MIR: Management International Review*: 123–147; Dunning JH and Lundan SM (2009) The internationalization of corporate R&D: A review of the evidence and some policy implications for home countries 1. *Review of Policy Research*, 26(1–2): 13–33; Iammarino S and McCann P (2013) *Multinationals and Economic Geography: Location, Technology and Innovation*. Cheltenham: Edward Elgar.

[e] Bertoni F, Elia S and Rabbiosi L (2013) Outward FDI from the BRICs: Trends and patterns of acquisitions in advanced countries. In M Marinov and S Marinova (eds.), *Emerging Economies and Firms in the Global Crisis*, pp. 47–82. Berlin: Springer; Buckley PJ, Clegg LJ and Cross AR (2015) The determinants of Chinese outward foreign direct investment. In P Buckley and P Ghauri (eds.), *International Business Strategy*, pp. 588–614. Abingdon: Routledge; Disdier A-C and Mayer T (2004) How different is Eastern Europe? Structure and determinants of location choices by French firms in Eastern and Western Europe. *Journal of Comparative Economics*, 32(2): 280–296; World Bank (2020), see Reference 18.

[f]Cadestin et al. (2018), see Reference 22.

[g]Disdier and Mayer (2004), see Reference 48e.

[h]World Bank (2020), see Reference 18.

49 Gereffi et al. (2005), see Reference 42.

50 Galvin P and Morkel A (2001) The effect of product modularity on industry structure: The case of the world bicycle industry. *Industry and Innovation*, 8(1): 31–47.

51 Gereffi and Fernandez-Stark (2016), see Reference 2.

52 Ponte and Sturgeon (2014), see Reference 43.

53 Forsgren M, Holm U and Johanson J (2007) *Managing the Embedded Multinational: A Business Network View*. Cheltenham: Edward Elgar; Dicken P (2015) *Global Shift: Mapping the Changing Contours of the World Economy*. New York: Guilford.

54 Cadestin et al. (2018), see Reference 2.

55 Krugman P (2007) The "new" economic geography: Where are we? In M. Fujita (ed.), *Regional Integration in East Asia*, pp. 23–34. Springer.

56 Cadestin et al. (2018), see Reference 2.

57 Cadestin et al. (2018), see Reference 2.

58 Dunning JH (1988) *Explaining International Production*. Collins Educational.

59 Dunning JH and Lundan SM (2008) *Multinational Enterprises and the Global Economy*. Cheltenham: Edward Elgar; Aldonas G (2013) *Trade Policy in a Global Age. E15 Initiative*. ICTSD and World Economic Forum (WEF).

60 Elms DK and Low P (2013) *Global Value Chains in a Changing World*. WTO/FGI/TFCTN.

61 Gould DM (2018) *Critical Connections: Promoting Economic Growth and Resilience in Europe and Central Asia*. Washington, DC: World Bank Publ.

62 Bailey et al. (2018), see Reference 5.

63 World Bank (2020), see Reference 18.

64 Gereffi G (2009) Development models and industrial upgrading in China and Mexico. *European Sociological Review*, 25(1): 37–51. doi:10.1093/esr/jcn034.

65 Cantwell J, Dunning JH and Lundan SM (2010) An evolutionary approach to understanding international business activity: The co-evolution of MNEs and the institutional environment. *Journal of International Business Studies*, 41(4): 567–586.

66 Giroud A and Mirza H (2015) Refining of FDI motivations by integrating global value chains' considerations. *Multinational Business Review*, 23(1): 67–76.

67 Giroud and Mirza (2015), see Reference 66.

68 Prasad E, Kenneth R, Shang-Jin W and Kose MA (2005) Effects of financial globalization on developing countries: Some empirical evidence. In W Tseng and D Cowen (eds.), *India's and China's Recent Experience with Reform and Growth*, pp. 201–228. London: Palgrave Macmillan.

69 World Bank (2020), see Reference 18.

70 Prasad et al. (2005), see Reference 68.

71 Morgan K (2004) The exaggerated death of geography: Learning, proximity and territorial innovation systems. *Journal of Economic Geography*, 4(1): 3–21.

72 Jordaan JA (2009) *Foreign Direct Investment, Agglomeration and Externalities: Empirical Evidence from Mexican Manufacturing Industries*. Farnham: Ashgate.

73 Crescenzi R, Pietrobelli C and Rabellotti R (2014) Innovation drivers, value chains and the geography of multinational corporations in Europe. *Journal of Economic Geography*, 14(6): 1053–1086. doi:10.1093/jeg/lbt018.

74 WTO (n.d.) WTO *"Trade in Value-Added and Global Value Chains" Profiles—Explanatory Notes*. Geneva: WTO.

75 Koopman R, Wang Z and Wei S-J (2014) Tracing value-added and double counting in gross exports. *American Economic Review*, 104(2): 459–494.

76 Taglioni D and Winkler D (2014), see Reference 30.

77 Koopman R, Powers W, Wang Z and Wei S-J (2010) *Give Credit Where Credit is Due: Tracing Value Added in Global Production Chains* (Working Paper Series No. 16426). Cambridge, MA: National Bureau of Economic Research (NBER).

78 United Nations Conference on Trade and Development (UNCTAD) (2018) *World Investment Report 2018: Investment and New Industrial Policies*. UNCTAD.

79 WTO (2019) *Technological Innovation, Supply Chain Trade, and Workers in a Globalised World. Global Value Chain Development Report 2019*. Geneva: WTO.

80 World Bank (2020), see Reference 18.

81 Pahl S and Timmer MP (2019) Do global value chains enhance economic upgrading? A long view. *Journal of Development Studies*, 1–23. doi:10.1080/00220388.2019.1702159.

82 World Bank (2020), see Reference 18.

83 Pahl and Timmer (2019), see Reference 81.

84 Gereffi (1995), see Reference 42; Gereffi et al. (2011), see Reference 6.

85 OECD (2019) *OECD Regional Outlook 2019: Leveraging Megatrends for Cities and Rural Areas*. Paris: OECD Publ.

86 OECD (2019), see Reference 85.

87 Bailey et al. (2018), see Reference 5.

88 Gereffi (2009), see Reference 64.

89 Foray D (2014) *Smart Specialisation: Opportunities and Challenges for Regional Innovation Policy*. Abingdon: Routledge.

90 Todeva E and Rakhmatullin R (2016) Industry global value chains, connectivity and regional Smart Specialisation in Europe. In *An Overview of Theoretical Approaches and Mapping Methodologies* (No. JRC102801). Seville: Joint Research Centre (JRC).

91 UNCTAD (2018), see Reference 78.

92 Echandi R (2015) *Connecting the Dots between International Trade & Investment Regulation, Investment Climate Reform & Development: The World Bank's Investment Reform Map*. Washington, DC: World Bank.

93 Fernandez-Arias E, Hausmann R and Stein E (2001) *Courting FDI: Is Competition Bad?* (Mimeo). Washington, DC: Inter-American Development Bank.

94 Crescenzi et al. (2014), see Reference 73.

95 Fuller C (2005) Corporate repeat investment and regional institutional capacity: The case of after-care services in Wales. *European Urban and Regional Studies*, 12(1): 5–21.

96 Alcácer J and Chung W (2007) Location strategies and knowledge spillovers. *Management Science*, 53(5): 760–776; OECD (2011) *Global Value Chains: Preliminary Evidence and Policy Issues. DSTI/IND*. Paris: OECD Publ.

97 Humphrey and Schmitz (2002), see Reference 23.

98 Cadestin et al. (2018), see Reference 2.

99 Borin A, Mancini M and Taglioni D (2021) *Measuring Exposure to Risk in Global Value Chains* (Policy Research Working Paper No. 9785). Washington, DC: World Bank.

100 As defined by Hummels D, Ishii J and Yi K-M (2001) The nature and growth of vertical specialization in world trade. *Journal of International Economics*, 54(1): 75–96. https://doi.org/10.1016/S0022-1996(00)00093-3.

101 Cadestin et al. (2018), see Reference 2.

102 Crescenzi R and Iammarino S (2017) Global investments and regional development trajectories: The missing links. *Regional Studies*, 51(1): 97–115. https://doi.org/10.1080/00343404.2016.1262016

103 Crescenzi R and Jaax A (2017) Innovation in Russia: The territorial dimension. *Economic Geography*, 93(1): 66–88.

104 Behuria S and Khullar R (1994) *Intermediate Services and Economic Development: The Malaysian Example* (E. O. Papers). Manila, Philippines: Asian Development Bank.

105 Calì M, Francois J, Hollweg CH, Manchin M, Oberdabernig DA, Rojas-Romagosa H, Rubinova S and Tomberger P (2016) *The Labor Content of Exports Database*. Washington, DC: World Bank.

106 De Marchi V, Di Maria E and Gereffi G (2017) *Local Clusters in Global Value Chains: Linking Actors and Territories Through Manufacturing and Innovation*. Abingdon: Routledge.

107 Lederman D and Maloney W (2012) *Does What You Export Matter? In Search of Empirical Guidance for Industrial Policies*. Washington, DC: World Bank.

108 Rodriguez-Clare A (2007) *Productive Development Policies and Supporting Institutions in Latin America and the Caribbean* (The State of State Reform in Latin America, Working Paper No. 106). Washington DC: IADB Research Department.

109 World Bank (2020), see Reference 18.

110 OECD (2018) *Productivity and Jobs in a Globalised World: (How) Can All Regions Benefit?* Paris: OECD Publ.

111 Choi J, Fukase E and Zeufack AG (2021) Global value chain participation, competition, and markups evidence from Ethiopian manufacturing firms. *Journal of Economic Integration*, 36(3): 491–517.

112 World Bank (2020), see Reference 18.

113 Gereffi G (2014) Global value chains in a post-Washington consensus world. *Review of International Political Economy*, 21(1): 9–37.

114 Taglioni and Winkler (2016), see Reference 76.

115 Gereffi et al. (2011), see Reference 6; Gereffi and Fernandez-Stark (2016), see Reference 22.

116 Taglioni and Winkler (2016), see Reference 76.

117 Gereffi, G (2005), The global economy: Organization, governance and development. In NJ Smelser and R Swedberg (eds.), *The Handbook of Economic Sociology*, 2nd edn, pp. 160–182, at 171. Princeton, NJ: Princeton University Press and Russell Sage Foundation.

118 Humphrey, J and Schmitz H (2002) How does insertion in global value chains affect upgrading in industrial clusters? *Regional Studies* 36(9): 1017-1027.

119 See Fernandez-Stark, K, Bamber, P and Gereffi, G (2011) The offshore services value chain: upgrading trajectories in developing countries. *International Journal of Technological Learning, Innovation and Development* **4**(1-3): 206-234.

120 See for example Frederick, SE (2010) Development and application of a value chain research approach to understand and evaluate internal and external factors and relationships affecting economic competitiveness in the textile value chain Ph.D., North Carolina State University. and Gereffi, G., S. Frederick and G. Gereffi (2010) *The global apparel value chain, trade and the crisis: challenges and opportunities for developing countries*, World Bank Washington, DC.

121 Humphrey, J. and H. Schmitz (2002). How does insertion in global value chains affect upgrading in industrial clusters? *Regional Studies* **36**(9): 1017-1027.

122 Gereffi G (2005) Export-oriented growth and industrial upgrading: Lessons from the Mexican apparel case: a case study of global value chains analysis. Available from the author.

3. How to upgrade through regional policy: building GVCs through FDI

Keywords: internationalisation; location choice ; linkages; Greenfield; FDI; global value chains; GVCs; mergers and acquisitions; M&A; investment

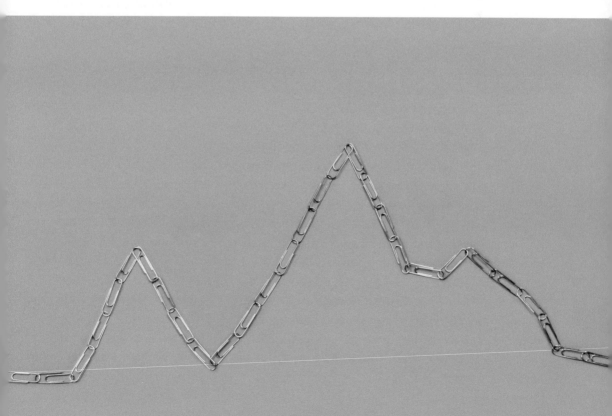

Key messages

- In building links with global value chains (GVCs), tying onto multinational enterprise (MNE) internationalisation efforts is critical for potential innovation benefits
- MNEs can build GVC linkages with the regional economy through both merger and acquisition (M&A) and greenfield investments
- Both national- and regional-level conditions matter for regions to link up to GVCs through foreign direct investment (FDI)
- There is no one-size-fits-all recipe for success. Location choices depend simultaneously on (1) the characteristics of the investing company (including its own "home" regional environment), (2) the nature of the investment (including its GVC position/stage) and (3) the characteristics of the host region
- Building institutional bridges and the subsequent reduction of cognitive distance between local actors and foreign companies is core to facilitate the matching of the "right" firms in the "right" regions in a highly assorted environment

For a region, building the link to the GVC is the crucial first step in using it for regional benefit. This building relies on certain location factors. Without that connection, regions remain unlinked to the chain, unable to embed or reshape for local value creation. Since **MNEs build GVCs through their actions, they are integral in this process**. More specifically, one of the first ways to build GVCs is through internationalisation efforts, that is, as MNEs delocalise activities beyond national borders. Regional policy decision-makers can leverage these locational factors to attract FDI and help connect the region to the GVC.

The attention placed on the locational factors of host economies has changed. This is due to recent trends in the types of activities that MNEs are moving abroad through FDI. MNEs have moved from locating less knowledge-intensive activities, such as standardised production outside of their home country,[1] to locating more knowledge-intensive activities and sophisticated business functions on foreign shores. An example is the inclusion of increasingly autonomous research and development (R&D) units in foreign subsidiaries. Thus, new ways of spreading innovation are delivered abroad through cross-border R&D activities.[2] China exemplifies this—its openness to FDI and number of high-quality engineers resulted in 50 MNE R&D centres in 1997 exploding to 600 by 2004.[3] These FDI knowledge flows are still very spatially concentrated at a subnational level.[4] As more complex activities relocate abroad, regions can connect to different parts of GVCs and build competitive advantage on fine-grained specialism. The new knowledge connections and increasing knowledge flows subsequently stimulate the development activity within the region.[5] They also tend to create good jobs with foreign affiliates generally paying higher wages relative to domestic ones. This is particularly evident in developing countries with the increase ranging from 10% to 70%. Much of this is due to **higher productivity of**

Regional Studies Policy Impact Books
© 2023 Riccardo Crescenzi and Oliver Harman
https://doi.org/10.1080/2578711X.2022.2099167

MNEs, leading to higher profits and an ability to pay higher wages.[6] In Lesotho and Madagascar, foreign-owned firms were instrumental in integrating production apparel export industries into GVCs.[7] This stimulation is not a one-off either, as the benefits of foreign ownership drive a continuous supply of headquarter services from the parent company to regional subsidiary.[8] Firms that are partially foreign owned, involving both foreign and local partnerships, are most likely to share technology with local suppliers and improve local productivity.[9] The foreign knowledge aspect is critical, because performance drops if foreign-owned firms are sold to local owners.[10] **Losing the international link can be bad for business.** It can also be bad for the transfer of knowledge and therefore the regional innovation system.

A growing body of evidence looks at the major regional influences in the relocation of different business functions of MNEs.[11] Less has been explicitly undertaken on knowledge and innovation factors and on how location drivers vary according to the value chain stages of activities.[12] Understanding the variation of investment drivers along the stages of the value chain is a necessary first step to designing working value chain-orientated policy.

3.1 WHAT IS DRIVING MNE DECISION-MAKING AND HOW CAN SUBNATIONAL POLICY ATTRACT THEIR CROSS-BORDER ACTIVITIES?

As outlined previously, the ownership, location and internationalisation (OLI) framework provides a general understanding of the three types of advantages that drive firms' internationalisation. When viewing this framework from a regional perspective (with the caveats discussed above with reference to GVC thinking), it is the "L" or location that matters and that policy decision-makers will try to influence. "L" is not only the host country but also the institutional and functional region as discussed above. This is the factor that links MNEs to a spatial unit, and that regional policy and regional socio-economic fundamentals can affect. Crucially, **the internationalisation process involves optimal matching between the characteristics and advantages of firms and locations**. This process—traditionally conceptualised and analysed at the national level—is fundamentally shaped by both national and subnational factors.[13]

New management and strategy work attempts to combine firm and location characteristics into a joint framework; specifically, the internal and external drivers of location choices.[14] Internal drivers are those within the firm. These drivers lead to firms **co-locating activities within locations**. External drivers are those outside of the firm. These drivers **push firms to locate activities in new locations**. The exploration of these forces takes place domestically, but the reasoning can apply to the international expansion of firms' activities. Consequently, we can understand international location decisions of different functions as the balance between internal and external drivers. This balance applies to the most sophisticated and the more routine activities. Both drivers consider firm and location variation in organising the value chain in space at the same time.[15]

There are different ways that firms looking to internationalise can enter a foreign market. The study of this choice is vast in international management[16] and international economics.[17] A commonly explored part within the entry mode literature—of special relevance for its local and regional development implications—looks at the "foreign establishment mode choice",[18] which consists of two main entry modes for equity investments:

1) **Firms can enter new countries and regions through M&A.** An acquisition involves a partial or full equity purchasing and, therefore, ownership of an existing firm.[19]

2) **Firms can enter foreign markets through greenfield investments.** This choice means building an entirely new subsidiary or establishment, with the subsidiary being either a joint venture with another company with complementary assets or a wholly owned subsidiary by the MNE.[20]

The entry mode choice depends on the characteristics of the investing MNE and characteristics of the host national and regional economy. Most evidence explores the host economy at the national level, with less known at the subnational level. **Both show firm characteristics matter.** For example, with US firms, it is argued that greenfield is generally favoured over acquisitions when the parent firm is more efficient, the host country is less developed and when there is closer geographical proximity between the parent firm and the host economy.[21]

If this is not the case, the firm might choose to acquire an existing company.

The foreign entry mode chosen by MNEs may have significant implications for the GVC since it changes the composition of firms in a region. From a GVC perspective, greenfield investments—FDI facilitating the establishment of new operations in a country via a subsidiary—are useful because the creation of new economic activity can help connect different activities, economic actors and regions. These connections ultimately help build GVC connectivity. Investments can also take place in the form of M&A. However, much less is known in the literature about the regional drivers of such investment and their impacts are more ambiguous in terms local economies. Acquisitions are only favourable to the local economy if the acquisition involves the transfer of new capital, knowledge and management practices to the newly acquired company. For more evident lessons, the rest of this section will, therefore, focus on greenfield investments as a tool for building GVCs. Discussion of the role of other (regional) entry modes will occur when looking at regional impacts.

3.2 WHAT FACTORS MATTER FOR ATTRACTING GVC INVESTMENT FLOWS?

Greenfield investments represent a type of FDI that provides a high degree of interfirm connectivity and high trust exchanges for the MNE,[22] also known as "relational governance".[23] The evidence converges on a set of crucial factors when looking at these FDI location decisions and, therefore, the built GVC link. These factors are three-fold:

1) Factors on the **location side**: that of the host region to FDI and the home region to FDI.

2) Factors of the **investor side**: that of the investing company.

3) Factors of the **investment side**: that of the new activity being created abroad.

Location side:

- A large body of evidence suggests that **institutions and related governance matters**.[24] Evidence shows that it is the host country's institutional quality[25] that is a vital location driver of FDI. Bureaucracy and corruption have particular prominence. The results provide a sense that **raising the quality of institutions and, in particular, converging them towards those of FDI source countries may help the receipt of flows**. This outcome may be necessary for lagging regions to note in their pursuit of FDI flows and building that link to the GVC.

- Location factors are at play for both national and regional levels. However, most of the literature has focused on the former. Accounting for the regional level can bring in another dimension of variation and matching specialisms. What matters—beyond agglomeration economies and density which also matter for domestic activities—are mostly soft factors that have to do with regional systems of innovation and more generally with favourable socio-economic conditions that form the profile of an "innovation prone" regional economy.[26]

- More recent studies find the subnational dimension of the location factor matters particularly for the model of entry by MNE—specifically whether the FDI is in the form of greenfield investment or acquisition. The regional quality of government makes a fundamental difference to the nature of the investment projects attracted by regions: those with high quality of government can attract greenfield investments undertaken by the most productive MNEs. By improving their quality of government, local and regional policy makers can attract higher quality FDI to their constituencies, potentially breaking the vicious circle between low productivity areas and low productivity FDI.[27]

Investor side:

- On the side of the investing company, **firm characteristics also affect the local attractiveness of regional economies**. There is, for example, variation in choices based on the R&D expenditure levels of investing companies.[28] Some firms that have low levels of in-house R&D expenditure tend to invest in locations where there is a high industrial innovative activity. On the contrary, those firms in which high levels of R&D expenditure already exist are attracted to locations with high levels of academic activity, but not necessarily industrial activity. They want to distance themselves from competitors and avoid the possible cost of outward spillovers.[29] Finally, higher productivity and innovative MNEs are more likely both to choose greenfield FDI and to do so in more innovative regional destinations.[30]

- In addition, the firm's ownership matters. For example, state-owned MNEs place less weight on the political risk of a host economy.[31] State-owned Chinese MNEs are, for instance, more concerned with favourable exchange rates than private Chinese MNEs. Hence **firm characteristics and strategies influence locational preferences for MNEs**.[32]

- The "home country" of the MNE matters, specifically on cases where MNEs are from emerging economies (EMNEs). The assumption is that firms are partly a function of where they originate. Here, using characteristics of the home region to proxy for firm characteristics is beneficial. There is an agreement that MNEs from advanced countries possess different features to MNEs from emerging countries.[33] Since their characteristics partly determine MNEs' location choices, MNEs from advanced countries may prefer different locations to MNEs from emerging countries.[34]

- This preference is revealed when EMNEs are particularly motivated to internationalise to access strategic assets. Such an asset may be superior knowledge[35] that is not domestically available.[36] Subsequently, EMNEs undertake explorative investments in the hope of catching up with global leaders in the field,[37] thereby improving their global competitiveness. Studies understanding the location choices of EMNEs at the regional level look at greenfield investments into the EU regions. It is found that when EMNEs are conducting innovation-related activities abroad, **European Union regions with high technological capabilities draw them in most significantly.**[38] Further to this, EMNEs tend to locate where there are other MNEs present and engaged in the same type of activity. Building a GVC with one EMNE is likely to lead to others. This co-location means that they can maximise their learning due to proximity to similar companies. The cognitive distance is lower than would be with advanced economies MNEs.

Investment side:

- It may not only be the characteristics of the firm that affect locational decisions. Instead, it may be the **types of activities within the chain that the company performs**.[39] The type of investment in terms of function and GVC stage is very important in understanding how firms are matched to different locations. When looking at EU regions, results suggest that for the most sophisticated knowledge-intensive stages of the value chain, regional socio-economic conditions are critically important for firms' decision-making. These soft factors at play show that national and regional levels perform different roles, and this is particularly true when considering the organisation of the value chain and the role of MNE subsidiaries.[40]

The emerging empirical picture from locational factors is that differences with firms and their particular activity type of interest is crucial. This is also the case with formal economic institutions; differences in firm choice are still critical, emphasising how important it is for decision-makers **to understand their socio-institutional fundamentals when looking at building the GVC**.

> **Case study 2: Penang Skills Development Centre (PSDC), Malaysia[41]**
>
> The PSDC is an example of reducing the distance between what firms want and what the location provides. The centre's creation allowed the region to build a workforce with industry-specific skills. Critically, it was firm and industry driven, responding to needs in human capital development in order to continue attracting global investment flows and building GVCs. Facilitated by subnational government, both Malaysian and foreign companies designed training programmes for their needs, continually updating them, allowing training to match tasks. Upgrading skills is necessary to export more advanced or higher value-added goods and services.
>
> The PSDC has more than 200 members and is a non-profit. Funding is fully provided through companies paying to send employees for training. Its success is clear in its delivery (200,000 workers taking more than 10,000 courses), and its adaptation (seeing replication throughout Malaysia).
>
> The knowledge provided is critical to regional decision-makers for three key reasons:
>
> 1) It helps attract and build global investment flows since it provides an enhanced technological environment
> 2) It removes informational bottlenecks and large mismatches in worker demand and supply
> 3) It keeps skills training local, adaptive and applicable—allowing advantage in engaging MNEs

The Penang case highlights the centrality of the human resource base in building GVCs through FDI. This high human capital is also positively correlated with GVC participation.[42] In order to modernise local industry, it is critical for regional policy decision-makers to continue upgrading skills and production capabilities[43] both in regionally present industries and those promoted for the future. Upgrading the workforce supports a shift in economic activity, moving towards high value-added areas of economic tasks. Addressing the ability to do this through education and training policy requires increased and continued life-long learning.[44]

3.3 VARYING DRIVERS OF LOCATION CHOICE

In summary, there are several various drivers of location choices when building GVCs through FDI. The split of sources is between the firm, the home region and the host region:

- Firm drivers refer to the set of firm characteristics that create their locational preferences. These can include the pre-existing geographical footprint of the firm, the firm's technological capabilities, the pursued entry mode and even the country of origin. Where the firm originates is particularly important to account for and is often used to stylise and proxy for characteristics internal to the firm. These sets of explicit and stylised firm characteristics can generate different locational preferences for investments.

- The characteristics of host regions are fundamental drivers in determining where MNEs decide to locate their investments. MNEs study institutions of host economies as a way of determining the types of locations in which MNEs prefer to invest. Another key host region driver is the technological environment provided. Some MNEs seek to locate in highly technological environments, while others may locate lower value-added tasks that may not require this.

Sources that affect choices of investment for building GVCs occur at both the firm and locational level. They interact with each other and both influence preferences regarding location choices. There is no one-size-fits-all approach, but matching firm characteristics with location characteristics is the most useful place to begin.

NOTES

1 Dunning JH (1996) *The Geographical Sources of the Competitiveness of Firms: Some Results of a New Survey*. University of Reading, Department of Economics Reading.
2 Schmitz H and Strambach S (2009) The organisational decomposition of innovation and global distribution of innovative activities: Insights and research agenda. *International Journal of Technological Learning, Innovation and Development*, 2(4): 231–249.
3 Freeman RB (2006) Does globalization of the scientific/engineering workforce threaten U.S. economic leadership? *Innovation Policy and the Economy*, 6: 123–157. doi:10.1086/ipe.6.25056182.
4 Crescenzi R and Harman O (2022) *Climbing Up Global Value Chains: Leveraging FDI for Economic Development* (Report). Hinrich Foundation. https://www.hinrichfoundation.com/research/wp/fdi/global-value-chains-gvc-foreign-direct-investment-fdi-economic-development/.
5 Grossman GM and Helpman E (1993) *Innovation and Growth in the Global Economy*. MIT Press.
6 Javorcik B (2019) *Eight Things Development Professionals Should Know about Foreign Direct Investment*. PEDL Synthesis Series, Private Enterprise Development in Low-Income Countries. Washington, DC: Center for Economic and Policy Research.
7 Morris M and Staritz C (2014) Industrialization trajectories in Madagascar's export apparel industry: Ownership, embeddedness, markets, and upgrading. *World Development*, 56: 243–257.
8 Javorcik (2019), see Reference 6.
9 World Bank. (2020) *World Development Report 2020: Trading for Development in the Age of Global Value Chains*. Washington, DC: World Bank.
10 Javorcik B and Poelhekke S (2017) Former foreign affiliates: Cast out and outperformed? *Journal of the European Economic Association*, 15(3): 501–539.
11 Defever F (2006) Functional fragmentation and the location of multinational firms in the enlarged Europe. *Regional Science and Urban Economics*, 36(5): 658–677.

12 Crescenzi R (2021) Changes in economic geography theory and the dynamics of technological change. In MM Fischer and P Nijkamp (eds.), *Handbook of Regional Science*, pp. 1307–1324. Berlin: Springer. https://doi.org/10.1007/978-3-642-23430-9_35

13 For national, see Ascani A, Crescenzi R and Iammarino S (2016) Economic institutions and the location strategies of European multinationals in their geographic neighborhood. *Economic Geography*, 92(4): 401–429; and for the subnational, see McCann P and Mudambi R (2005) Analytical differences in the economics of geography: The case of the multinational firm. *Environment and Planning A*, 37(10): 1857–1876.

14 Alcacer J and Delgado M (2016) Spatial organization of firms and location choices through the value chain. *Management Science*, 62(11): 3213–3234. https://doi.org/10.1287/mnsc.2015.2308

15 Bruno RL, Crescenzi R, Estrin S and Petralia S (2021) Multinationals, innovation, and institutional context: IPR protection and distance effects. *Journal of International Business Studies*. doi:10.1057/s41267-021-00452-z.

16 Werner S (2002) Recent developments in international management research: A review of 20 top management journals. *Journal of Management*, 28(3): 277–305.

17 Nocke V and Yeaple S (2008) An assignment theory of foreign direct investment. *Review of Economic Studies*, 75(2): 529–557.

18 Cho KR and Padmanabhan P (1995) Acquisition versus new venture: The choice of foreign establishment mode by Japanese firms. *Journal of International Management*, 1(3): 255–285.

19 Barkema HG and Vermeulen F (1998) International expansion through start-up or acquisition: A learning perspective. *Academy of Management Journal*, 41(1): 7–26.

20 Buckley PJ and Ghauri PN (2004) Globalisation, economic geography and the strategy of multinational enterprises. *Journal of International Business Studies*, 35(2): 81–98. https://doi.org/10.1057/palgrave.jibs.8400076; Cooke P (2013) *Complex Adaptive Innovation Systems: Relatedness and Transversality in the Evolving Region*. Abingdon: Routledge.

21 Nocke and Yeaple (2008), see Reference 17.

22 Gereffi G, Humphrey J and Sturgeon T (2005) The governance of global value chains. *Review of International Political Economy*, 12(1): 78–104. https://doi.org/10.1080/09692290500049805

23 Zaheer A and Venkatraman N (1995) Relational governance as an interorganizational strategy: An empirical test of the role of trust in economic exchange. *Strategic Management Journal*, 16(5): 373–392.

24 Globerman S and Shapiro D (2002) Global foreign direct investment flows: The role of governance infrastructure. *World Development*, 30(11): 1899–1919.

25 Bénassy-Quéré A, Coupet M and Mayer T (2007) Institutional determinants of foreign direct investment. *World Economy*, 30(5): 764–782.

26 Crescenzi R, Pietrobelli C and Rabellotti R (2014) Innovation drivers, value chains and the geography of multinational corporations in Europe. *Journal of Economic Geography*, 14(6): 1053–1086. doi:10.1093/jeg/lbt018.

27 Amendolagine V, Crescenzi R and Rabellotti R (2022) The geography of acquisitions and greenfield investments: firm heterogeneity and regional institutional conditions. Geography and Environment Discussion Paper Series (33). Department of Geography and Environment, LSE, London, UK. http://eprints.lse.ac.uk/115597/

28 Alcácer J and Chung W (2007) Location strategies and knowledge spillovers. *Management Science*, 53(5): 760–776.

29 Crescenzi R, Dyèvre A and Neffke F (2022) Innovation catalysts: How multinationals reshape the global geography of innovation. *Economic Geography*, 98: 199–227. doi:10.1080/00130095.2022.20 26766.

30 Amendolagine et al. (2022), see Reference 27.

31 Duanmu J-L (2012) Firm heterogeneity and location choice of Chinese multinational enterprises (MNEs). *Journal of World Business*, 47(1): 64–72.

32 Helpman E, Melitz MJ and Yeaple SR (2004) Export versus FDI with heterogeneous firms. *American Economic Review*, 94(1): 300–316. doi:10.1257/000282804322970814; Buch CM, Kleinert J, Lipponer A, Toubal F and Baldwin R (2005) Determinants and effects of foreign direct investment: Evidence from German firm-level data. *Economic Policy*, 20(41): 52–110; Cantwell J (2009) Location and the multinational enterprise. *Journal of International Business Studies*, 40(1): 35–41.

33 Kumar K and McLeod MG (1981) *Multinationals from Developing Countries*. Washington DC: Lexington Books; Lall S, Chen E, Katz J, Kosacoff B and Villela A (1983) *The New Multinationals: The Spread of Third World Enterprises*. Chichester, UK: Wiley.

34 Hyun JH (2008) How different are emerging multinationals' views of economic integration in Europe? A case study of Korean automobile manufacturers' strategic reactions. *European Planning Studies*, 16(6): 745–760; Cuervo-Cazurra A and Ramamurti R (2014) *Understanding Multinationals from Emerging Markets*. Cambridge: Cambridge University Press.

35 Ramamurti R (2012) What is really different about emerging market multinationals? *Global Strategy Journal*, 2(1): 41–47; Bertoni F, Elia S and Rabbiosi L (2013) Outward FDI from the BRICs: Trends and patterns of acquisitions in advanced countries. In M Marinov and S Marinova (eds.), *Emerging Economies and Firms in the Global Crisis*, pp. 47–82. London: Palgrave Macmillan.

36 Awate S, Larsen MM and Mudambi R (2015) Accessing vs sourcing knowledge: A comparative study of R&D internationalization between emerging and advanced economy firms. *Journal of International Business Studies*, 46(1): 63–86.

37 Dunning JH (1993) MNEs, the balance of payments and the structure of trade. In J Dunning and S Lundan (eds.), *Multinational Enterprises and the Global Economy*. Wokingham: Addison-Wesley; Meyer KE (2015) What is "strategic asset seeking FDI"? *Multinational Business Review*, 23(1): 57–66.

38 Crescenzi R, Pietrobelli C and Rabellotti R (2016) Regional strategic assets and the location strate-gies of emerging countries' multinationals in Europe. *European Planning Studies*, 24(4): 645–667. https://doi.org/10.1080/09654313.2015.1129395

39 Ascani, A., Crescenzi, R., Iammarino, S. (2016) Economic institutions and the location strategies of European multinationals in their geographical neighbourhood, *Economic Geography*, 92(4): 401–429. doi:10.1080/00130095.2016.1179570; Crescenzi (2021), see Reference 12.

40 Rugman A, Verbeke A and Yuan W (2011) Re-conceptualizing Bartlett and Ghoshal's classification of national subsidiary roles in the multinational enterprise. *Journal of Management Studies*, 48(2): 253–277.

41 Farole T (2011) *Special Economic Zones in Africa: Comparing Performance and Learning from Global Experience*. Washington, DC: World Bank.

42 Yameogo ND and Jammeh K (2019) *Determinants of Participation in Manufacturing GVCs in Africa: The Role of Skills, Human Capital Endowment, and Migration* (Policy Research Working Paper No. 8938). Washington, DC: World Bank. https://openknowledge.worldbank.org/handle/10986/32058

43 Organisation for Economic Co-operation and Development (OECD) (2019) *Regions in Industrial Transition: Policies for People and Places*. Paris: OECD Publ. https://www.oecd.org/publications/regions-in-industrial-transition-c76ec2a1-en.htm

44 OECD (2007) *Moving Up the Value Chain: Staying Competitive in the Global Economy*. Paris: OECD Publ. https://www.oecd.org/industry/ind/stayingcompetitiveintheglobaleconomymovingup thevaluechainsynthesisreport.htm

4. How to upgrade through regional policy: embedding GVCs through FDI

Keywords: global value chains; GVCs; upgrading; offshoring; innovation; technology; investment

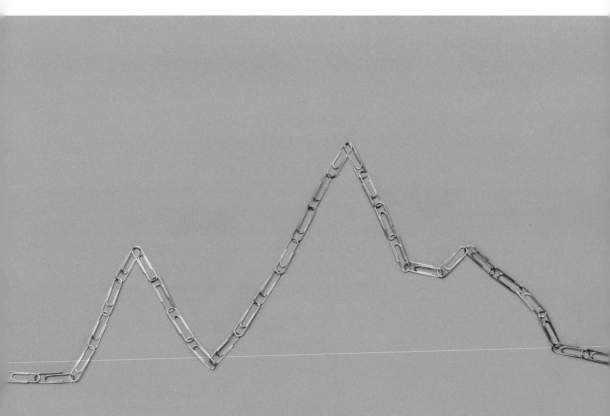

Key messages

- Regional embedding of global value chains (GVCs) can occur from both foreign firms bringing activities to the host region as well as domestic firms offshoring activities to other regions abroad
- Varying firms enter regions in different ways. Their effects on regional economies can be highly differentiated. Regional policy decision-makers must be cognisant of this in order to capture and embed knowledge spillovers and externalities
- Offshoring research and development (R&D) does not hurt innovation, which would otherwise be taking place at home. Instead, such international investments increase multinational enterprise (MNE) innovation in the home region
- A "proactive search" of new knowledge—that of policy driving active internationalisation of firms—is shown to be very effective. Regional policy decision-makers should not limit the international expansion of domestic firms by encouraging reshoring. By doing this they will miss out on beneficial knowledge streams
- A key challenge for public policy in less developed regions is how to facilitate collaboration, learning and upgrading by local firms from internationalised domestic and foreign companies

Once establishing the locational factors driving the link to the GVC through foreign direct investment (FDI), thought and policy must turn to embedding the MNE in the host economy. This embedding helps ensure knowledge and innovation impact. As MNEs have begun to delocalise varied functions, differing degrees of local embeddedness and linkages can occur.[1] The framing of regional impacts from embedding GVCs through FDI is in two ways:

1) Those that diffuse from foreign MNE activities in the host economy.
2) Those that can flow back to the "home" region from previously offshored foreign MNE activities.

Or, to put it another way, "to combine embedded and local assets with international sourcing and outsourcing".[2] The positive regional impacts do not just benefit the region receiving FDI, but also the region providing it. Figure 4.1 shows this benefit. Specifically, the proactive search for new knowledge in host regions sees firms tap into new innovative networks. This is then translated back to the home environment through intra-firm knowledge flows. These knowledge flows subsequently get shared and spill over to the host region via several mechanisms explained below.

Regional Studies Policy Impact Books
© 2023 Riccardo Crescenzi and Oliver Harman

https://doi.org/10.1080/2578711X.2022.2099169

Figure 4.1 Knowledge benefits of outsourcing

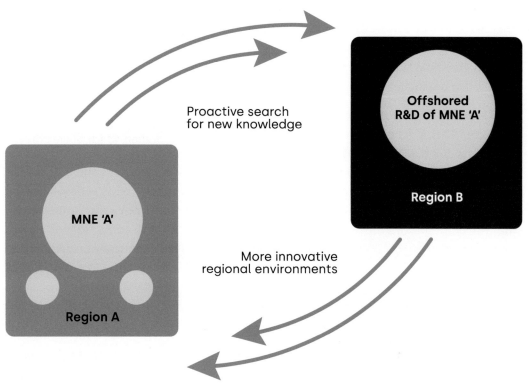

Source: Author's elaboration

Embedding GVCs into regions is described as a process of making them become "sticky places".[4] The role of subnational government is to help regions reinvigorate themselves. By changing their growth trajectory to one that is more dynamic, their activities will become more embedded and more challenging to shift elsewhere. GVCs are, after

> **What is a "sticky place"?**
>
> With advances in transportation and information, it is increasingly difficult for regions to anchor income-generating activities.
>
> A sticky place is building precisely this embeddedness, ensuring activities anchor in the region. Sticky places are complex products of multiple sources such as corporate strategies, industrial structures and local policy[3]

all, "embedded within local economic, social and institutional dynamics. Insertion in the GVC depends significantly on these local conditions".[5]

4.1 TECHNOLOGY DIFFUSION AND INNOVATION IN HOST REGION

MNEs are actors endowed with knowledge and technology. They are producers of knowledge,[6] with the top 100 companies representing a third of business-funded R&D worldwide.[7] With this, they tend to outperform the domestic counterparts in the host economy, which are typically less productive and innovative.[8]

When entering a new host economy, the inward FDI has the potential to act as an externality generator.[9] That is, its presence in a host economy brings benefits to wider firms and citizens. This is due to MNEs, unable to fully internalise knowledge and technology, create spillovers.[10] Therefore, positive impacts may accrue from a region tapping into the GVC via FDI. However, actual linkages between the foreign firm and local actors must be developed for local impacts to materialise; **FDI leading to GVC embeddedness is not a foregone conclusion**. The syndrome of a firm with limited local linkages from an MNE entry,[11] that of "branch plant", is always a possibility. Further, if the domestic sector is not adequately technologically advanced, potential knowledge flows will not be absorbed in the host region. This need of absorptive capacity, as examined previously, is an important consideration and can be aided with active public policy.[12] Reactive and responsive connections must occur for the MNE link to GVCs to work for the benefit of the host region.

There are specific mechanisms through which MNEs can impact host economies:[13]

- Demonstration effects: the behavioural change of individuals caused by observing the actions of others and their consequences.

- Competition effects: the change of firms processes or productivity caused by striving to compete with new competitors.

- Labour market effects: the change in supply and demand of labour and wages.

- Backward and forward linkages: the change in investment in facilities to enable project success or investment in subsequent stages of production, respectively.

These impacts are typically demonstrated through productivity,[14] employment[15] and innovation.[16] Recent studies explore the regional implications of MNEs' activities and their integration in GVCs. It is important to note that increased productivity may, in turn, facilitate a structural shift towards higher value-added activities, that of moving up the value chain.[17]

> **Case study 3: Local embedding of firms in Istanbul, Turkey[18]**
>
> Public and private subnational actors have coordinated work in order to successfully see Turkey embed firms, upgrade through the value cain, and build global brands. Beginning in production, firms are now assuming higher value design roles. This change has been driven through

subnational actors. First, the Istanbul Textile and Apparel Exporter Association (ITKIB) partnered with its firms and government agencies to upgrade its workforce with vocational training. ITKIB currently supports four vocational schools.[19] Furthermore, such subnational coordination resulted in the Small and Medium Industry Development Organisation (KOSGEB) changing its mandate. Initially, for production-based activities, the increase in added-value potential and demand for firms upgrading in the value chain[20] saw the organisation alter its mandate. It supported Istanbul firms with incentives such as reimbursing training for skills, recruiting for highly qualified personnel and R&D costs. Istanbul's Textile and Apparel Exported Association members now account for 12% of the country's export at US$17 billion annually,[21] and the case exemplifies the importance of public policy and investment with further examples shared elsewhere[22]

As highlighted previously, greenfield investments have crucial governance links with the MNE and the GVC. However, along with differences within types of firms embedding in the regional network, there are also varied entry modes. Evidence shows that the links that already exist through acquired firms may allow broader regional benefit and spillovers than new linkages through greenfield investment.[23] Looking at those differing links in Latin America, evidence shows greenfield investments are not the only type of investments regions should hope to attract.[24] **M&A investments—under the right conditions—can potentially offer a more direct channel for knowledge diffusion**, the relative importance of which depends on three elements:

1) The local conditions and efforts.

2) The GVC position of the country.

3) The GVC stage of the investment.

This direct channel is interesting as the importance of the subnational's input into the design of innovation policies is growing in Europe and also, for example, in Latin America.[25] With the GVC lens, **regional firms being on the receiving end of an M&A deal is not necessarily a negative outcome**. It is instead an opportunity for the creation of knowledge spillovers. This opportunity is because M&A shows a strong link between patenting and investments, suggesting that the prior embeddedness of M&A projects may better facilitate knowledge diffusion.[26]

Therefore, different types of firms enter the regional economy, but these also enter with different modes. The effects can be highly differentiated depending on investing company characteristics. On top of this, also specific regional factors determine the effect. It is this variation between the firm and the regional features that shapes impact.

4.2 CAN FIRMS OFFSHORING INVESTMENT ABROAD HELP HOME REGIONS?

Knowledge flows can also occur back to the regional economy via the GVC from outward connections elsewhere. The categorisation of these connections can **be either outsourcing or offshoring**. The key differences between the two are in the control over, and location of, the connected organisation. The choice of governance mode may provide different access advantages as well as organisation efficiency gains.[27] However, the importance of equity investments in our discussion means it is offshoring that is of primary interest.

This offshoring is a form of embeddedness, albeit of a different type. **The lead firm's connection to an offshore region allows the knowledge flow benefits.** This knowledge can come in the form of offshoring and co-location of both production and R&D—the latter being of most interest in the innovation story. Offshoring has a two-way nature. Offshoring from the providing region's perspective is the same as technology diffusion from the receiving region's perspective.

MNEs may take part in both goods and service offshorings. The former looks at the relocation of production activities such as assembly, while the latter looks at the relocation of service activities such as call centre operations, accounting and, key in the discussion on innovation, that of R&D.[28] The existing literature provides many motivating reasons for why MNEs might outsource their R&D. These fall into three principal categories:

- To support other stages of their value chain located in foreign markets.[29]
- To access knowledge that is otherwise unavailable to them in the domestic market.[30]
- To reduce the cost of their R&D investment by outsourcing, sharing fixed costs and relying on specialised providers.[31]

This frontier thinking provides the other side of the picture when thinking about regional embeddedness in the GVC. It should not only be the seeking of embedding GVCs at home that regional decision-makers should focus on, but also embedding those abroad. Connectivity benefits that may enhance the region can work both ways, and geographical proximity is not always necessary.[32]

When innovative activities relocate abroad, regional policy decision-makers should look at the potential to gain from them. This perspective contrasts with the typical viewpoint of it being a loss of innovative economic activity. Case study 4 shows how knowledge and technology from offshore investment can enhance regional innovation at home. Similarly, China's "go-out" policy (also known as the Going Global Strategy) is seen as a significant contributor to the country's growth over the past 20 years.[33] The policy stimulated domestic firms to invest internationally, which in turn built a foundation of high-technology industries.

https://doi.org/10.1080/2578711X.2022.2099169

This new outward FDI had a significant positive impact on technology innovation. To ensure its success, there was an important role played by provincial or regional governments to provide not only sufficient human capital and infrastructure but also local R&D capacity so regions could absorb the new knowledge.

Co-location between different parts of the value chain is another possibility for embedding the GVC. Firms locate different stages of their value chain near each other.[34] This pursuit of proximity is in the hope of saving on coordination costs and benefitting from complementarities. Related activities concentrate in the same country—close to each other. This is the case for R&D activities and production plants, which favour co-location strategies.[35] It is the geography of prior investments on which a firm's location decisions are mainly dependent, as firms in general tend to reinvest and thus co-locate in the same region in which they have invested previously. However, there is disparity along the value chain, that is, it is only the nearby location of production plants that is important for production activities.

Service activities, on the other hand, do not need such physical proximity to other functions. By looking at where co-location with production matters in GVCs, evidence shows that having prior manufacturing activities increases the probability of R&D investment following in the same location.[36] Furthermore, offshoring R&D does not hurt innovation that would be taking place at home otherwise. **Instead, such international investments have tended to increase MNE innovation activities in the home region**. They are complementary, and the knowledge flows across borders via the MNE network. There is a link between the foreign locational activities of MNEs and offshoring, but they are not the same. Offshoring does not take place only within MNE boundaries, and similarly, MNEs do not only pursue offshoring activities.[37] **What matters as much as co-location in space and geographical proximity is a combination of social, cultural and economic factors**. Together, these factors engender the trust-based and informal relations necessary for knowledge flows.[38]

This understanding addresses the policy concern that the offshoring of production activities will see innovative activities follow. There seems to be no direct "push" for firms to follow with innovative activities; instead, what occurs is a "pull" of foreign locations for R&D. This pull might be due to the offshoring of R&D tapping into knowledge pipelines otherwise unavailable to home regions and their firms. **The competitiveness of local production systems increasingly depends on their ability to combine and embed local assets with international sourcing and outsourcing**.[39]

Foreign market access and external knowledge are crucial policy tools at hand. This is partially due to MNEs' rising motivation to offshore R&D.[40] Initially, the focus was on innovation in terms of knowledge spillovers between geographically close actors in a local production network.[41] More recently, this discussion of innovation is in terms of translocal cooperation and externalities flowing across a different geographical scale.[42] Following this lead, evidence from 6000 French firms between 1999 and 2011 shows that the offshoring of R&D activities can be a useful tool for firms in accessing and exporting to previously untapped knowledge sources.[43] Similarly, a study in the United States shows that, at the regional level, there is a positive link between outward greenfield FDI and local employment. The benefit is particularly felt in less developed regions.[44] Without this connection, firms may be missing out on critical value abroad. But with it, **the region can capture benefits from active internationalisation, leveraging FDI to generate scale and productivity in the home region**.[45] It reemphasises the importance of how the **embedding of GVCs in a region can provide new trading opportunities, as opposed to focusing on domestic value chains**.

Case study 4: Knowledge benefits of offshoring—CEMEX, Mexico[46]

The cement and concrete producer CEMEX represents a useful case exemplifying internationalisation and subsequent knowledge flows.[47] The Mexican firm initially used offshore investment to enter new markets and gain production ability. It started investment with Spanish subsidiaries, and subsequently with Latin America and Caribbean affiliates. Today, the Mexican firm, like many of its peers, has gathered new technologies and innovative capacities through offshore investments in R&D centres or firms with higher technology expertise in more advanced regions.[48]

Policy decision-makers could have attempted to restrict this, citing the need for local jobs. However, the pursuit of more advanced activities with firms in more innovative regions underpins upgrading. It is the active pursuit of more advanced knowledge that brings benefits. Firms are less likely to develop along the value chain if they offshore to equally developed firms in similarly knowledgeable countries. Evidence shows that if firms do not pursue more advanced activities, the composition of skills at home does not significantly change.[49] This is likely because their scope to learn new skills and upgrade is lower

---

Moreover, evidence also comes from the United States looking at substate economic areas and innovative regional environments.[50] **As a result of increasing global connectivity, regions can develop new competitive local strategies and identify new trajectories for local development**.[51] This reconfiguration can happen predominantly through the access of externally generated inputs which are unavailable locally. It is also useful for GVC embedding, because when subsidiaries are embedded in their host regions' economies as well as in their global intra-firm networks, MNEs play the role of channelling knowledge across borders.[52]

To enhance these environments and subnational economic areas, a proactive search of new knowledge is most effective, that is, by following a policy of active internationalisation of firms. This matters more than any investment connections established domestically. Regional policy decision-makers should not limit the international expansion of domestic firms by encouraging reshoring. This limit could undermine the very thing they want by presenting an obstacle

https://doi.org/10.1080/2578711X.2022.2099169

to regional innovativeness and competitiveness. **There is a real danger that in pure promotion of domestic rather than GVCs, regions—both lagging and frontier—will miss out on essential knowledge streams and trade avenues**. Indeed, between 1996 and 2016, one in four persons in the Organisation for Economic Co-operation and Development (OECD) lived in a region falling further behind the high-productivity frontier.[53] Building and embedding links with GVCs driving upgrading is one way in which they can catch up.

4.3 VARYING DRIVERS OF IMPACT

The regional innovation impacts associated with the activities of foreign firms are highly varied. This diversity of impacts depends on various interrelated dimensions, which include:

- The characteristics of the investing company.
- The nature and objective of its investment, including its value chain stage.
- The characteristics of the host economy—from the macro- and national institutional environment through the regional and local innovation system down to the absorptive capacity of domestic firms.

These sources of difference are not independent of each other. They are bound by the strategic choices of firms, often under the influence of public policy. When reflecting on how regions can link up to value chains by embedding foreign investments, these sources of deviation become fundamentally important. **Embedding foreign activities generates highly diversified regional innovation impacts**. While there is evidence on these factors—albeit often in isolation—knowledge of their dynamic interaction is critical, and now receiving growing attention. For example, when looking at the characteristics of the investing companies, evidence suggests that firms aim at minimising knowledge leakages from their foreign activities whilst maximising their reliance on intra-firm knowledge sources.[54]

Following this, studies compare whether regions derive the most considerable innovation benefits from investments by the most highly innovative foreign companies, or if more medium-ranked innovative foreign investors might be more beneficial to their host. Evidence shows that **in aiming to attract foreign investment into their region and embed firms in the broader value chain, it is important to not fight for the big-name tech giants**.[55] These firms are, in fact, less likely to bring local benefit and generate local innovation on the whole. Technological giants are more effective at minimising knowledge leakages and have fewer incentives to interact with the local ecosystem. Furthermore, the cognitive gap between these highly innovative firms and local firms may be too large for any knowledge transfer. The local firms will stay primarily excluded from the GVC. Therefore, when seeking links with the GVC, **engagement should be with medium-ranked innovative foreign investors** in order to get the most significant innovation impact from the link. These firms might offer the highest local returns via labour circulation, collaboration and spillover effects.

There are some potential negative impacts of FDI worth emphasising. This harmful potential should serve as a warning to all regions, but particularly to those that are lagging. Technology may not transfer to and embed in all regions in the same way. Studies in transition economies show that unless direct equity affiliate links are being made, limited spillovers occur.[56] In some country cases, international R&D spillovers occur; however, in others, there is some crowding out of local firms in the same industry.[57] Yes, FDI in technology can boost innovation, but this often occurs only with domestic firms which already have a high level of innovation and can compete.[58] For those firms without this high level of innovation, it is likely that enterprise will not continue. Moreover, in some developing countries, firms participating in GVCs might be required to adopt new technologies to stay competitive. While productivity-enhancing, these technologies are ultimately labour-saving and may have consequences for jobs.[59] The effects and impacts of embeddedness thus vary considerably.

New technologies may also affect the balance between both positive and negative effects in different types of regions. **There are embeddedness impacts from the home region and embeddedness impacts from the host region. In the home region, varying linkages and technological diffusion provide different impacts. With the host, the new offshored connectivity brings new proximity**. The offshoring ties in the home region with potential new knowledge sources of the host region. The effects are therefore highly differentiated depending on the characteristics of the region and the investing company. Moreover, firms can undertake different types of investment in different entry modes that add another dimension of variation. It is the interplay between the company and regional features that ultimately shapes impacts.

With reference to embeddedness more generally, it does not always mean geographical proximity.[60] **It is not only co-location that matters. There is a role of concrete personal relations and networks in generating this human proximity**.[61] It is useful to embed GVC thinking in terms of a wider proximity framework[62] with the relational embedding of firms is a crucial element within regional networks. Systems rest on embedded and strong trustful socio-economic linkages,[63] and without this, there will be limited creation and diffusion of new knowledge.[64] Furthermore, without human or organisational proximity, any co-creation may not be able to be captured by the region or its citizens.[65]

NOTES

1 Dimitratos P, Liouka I and Young S (2009) Regional location of multinational corporation subsidiaries and economic development contribution: Evidence from the UK. *Journal of World Business*, 44(2): 180–191.

2   Propris LD, Menghinello S and Sugden R (2008) The internationalisation of production systems: embeddedness, openness and governance. *Entrepreneurship and Regional Development*, 20(6): 493–515.

3   Markusen A (1996) Sticky places in slippery space: A typology of industrial districts. *Economic Geography*, 72(3): 293–313. https://doi.org/10.2307/144402

4   Markusen (1996), see Reference 3; Bailey D, Pitelis C and Tomlinson PR (2018) A place-based developmental regional industrial strategy for sustainable capture of co-created value. *Cambridge Journal of Economics*, 42(6): 1521–1542. https://doi.org/10.1093/cje/bey019

5   Gereffi G and Fernandez-Stark K (2016) *Global Value Chain Analysis: A Primer*. Duke University. http://hdl.handle.net/10161/12488.

6   Javorcik B (2019) *Eight Things Development Professionals Should Know about Foreign Direct Investment*. PEDL Synthesis Series, Private Enterprise Development in Low-Income Countries. Washington, DC: Center for Economic and Policy Research.

7   United Nations Conference on Trade and Development (UNCTAD) (2019) *World Investment Report: Special Economic Zones*. UNCTAD. https://worldinvestmentreport.unctad.org/world-investment-report-2019/

8   Castellani D and Zanfei A (2006) *Multinational Firms, Innovation and Productivity*. Cheltenham: Edward Elgar; Criscuolo C, Haskel JE and Slaughter MJ (2010) Global engagement and the innovation activities of firms. *International Journal of Industrial Organization*, 28(2): 191–202.

9   Smarzynska Javorcik B (2004) Does foreign direct investment increase the productivity of domestic firms? In search of spillovers through backward linkages. *American Economic Review*, 94(3): 605–627. doi: 10.1257/0002828041464605; Xu X and Sheng Y (2012) Productivity spillovers from foreign direct investment: Firm-level evidence from China. *World Development*, 40(1): 62–74.

10 Markusen J (2005) *Modeling the Offshoring of White-Collar Services: From Comparative Advantage to the New Theories of Trade and FDI*. Cambridge, MA: National Bureau of Economic Research (NBER).

11 For an overview, see Hood N and Young S (1999) *The Globalization of Multinational Enterprise Activity and Economic Development*. Berlin: Springer; and for specific examples, see Phelps NA, Mackinnon D, Stone I and Braidford P (2003) Embedding the multinationals? Institutions and the development of overseas manufacturing affiliates in Wales and North East England. *Regional Studies*, 37(1): 27–40.

12 For a detailed discussion of absorptive capacity and public policy for GVCs, see Crescenzi R and Harman O (2022) *Climbing Up Global Value Chains: Leveraging FDI for Economic Development* (Report). Hinrich Foundation. https://www.hinrichfoundation.com/research/wp/fdi/global-value-chains-gvc-foreign-direct-investment-fdi-economic-development/.

13 For examples, evidence and discussion, see Blomström M and Kokko A (1998) Multinational corporations and spillovers. *Journal of Economic Surveys*, 12(3): 247–277; Görg H and Greenaway D (2004) Much ado about nothing? Do domestic firms really benefit from foreign direct investment? *World Bank Research Observer*, 19(2): 171–197; Smeets R (2008) Collecting the pieces of the FDI knowledge spillovers puzzle. *World Bank Research Observer*, 23: 107–138; Crescenzi R, Gagliardi L

and Iammarino S (2015) Foreign multinationals and domestic innovation: Intra-industry effects and firm heterogeneity. *Research Policy*, 44(3): 596–609.

14 For cross-country evidence, see Blomström and Kokko (1998), see Reference 13; and for country-specific evidence, see Aitken BJ and Harrison AE (1999) Do domestic firms benefit from direct foreign investment? Evidence from Venezuela. *American Economic Review*, 89(3): 605–618.

15 Cortinovis N, Crescenzi R and van Oort F (2020) Multinational enterprises, industrial relatedness and employment in European regions. *Journal of Economic Geography*, 20(5): 1165–1205. doi:10.1093/jeg/lbaa010.

16 Fu X (2008) Foreign direct investment, absorptive capacity and regional innovation capabilities: Evidence from China. *Oxford Development Studies*, 36(1): 89–110; Crescenzi et al. (2015), see Reference 13; Crescenzi R and Jaax A (2017) Innovation in Russia: The territorial dimension. *Economic Geography*, 93(1): 66–88. https://doi.org/10.1080/00130095.2016.1208532

17 Farole T and Winkler D (2014) *Making Foreign Direct Investment Work for Sub-Saharan Africa: Local Spillovers and Competitiveness in Global Value Chains*. Washington, DC: World Bank. http://hdl.handle.net/10986/16390

18 World Bank (2020) *World Development Report 2020: Trading for Development in the Age of Global Value Chains*. Washington, DC: World Bank. https://www.worldbank.org/en/publication/wdr2020

19 Ihkib (2020) *Istanbul Apparel Exporters Association*. http://www.ihkib.org.tr.

20 KOSGEB (2020) *Small and Medium Industries Development Organization (KOSGEB)*. https://www.devex.com/organizations/small-and-medium-industries-development-organization-kosgeb-120822.

21 Ihkib (2020), see Reference 19.

22 For detail on public policy and investment, see Crescenzi and Harman (2022), see Reference 12.

23 Chapman K (2003) Cross-border mergers/acquisitions: A review and research agenda. *Journal of Economic Geography*, 3(3): 309–334; Crespo N and Fontoura MP (2007) Determinant factors of FDI spillovers–what do we really know? *World Development*, 35(3): 410–425; Balsvik R and Haller SA (2010) Foreign firms and host-country productivity: Does the mode of entry matter? *Oxford Economic Papers*, 63(1): 158–186.

24 Crescenzi R and Jaax A (2022) Multinational enterprises and the geography of innovation in Latin America: Evidence from Brazil, Mexico, and Colombia.

25 Pietrobelli C and Rabellotti R (2006) Clusters and value chains in Latin America: In search of an integrated approach. In C Pietrobelli and R Rabellotti (eds.), *Upgrading to Compete: Global Value Chains, Clusters, and SMEs in Latin America*, 1–40. Cambridge, MA: Harvard University Press. https://ssrn.com/abstract=1551498; Sanguinetti P, Pineda J, Scandizzo S, Ortega D and Penfold M (2010) RED 2010: Local development: towards a new protagonism of cities and regions (ch. 1). Caracas: Corporacion Andina de Fomento (CAF). http://scioteca.caf.com/handle/123456789/941; Koeller P and Cassiolato JE (2011) *Achievements and Shortcomings of Brazil's Innovation Policies*. Londres: Anthem.

26 Crescenzi and Jaax (2022), see Reference 24.

27 Metters R (2008) A typology of offshoring and outsourcing in electronically transmitted services. *Journal of Operations Management*, 26(2): 198–211; Kedia BL and Mukherjee D (2009) Understanding

offshoring: A research framework based on disintegration, location and externalization advantages. *Journal of World Business*, 44(3): 250–261.

28 Crinò R (2009) Offshoring, multinationals and labour market: A review of the empirical literature. *Journal of Economic Surveys*, 23(2): 197–249.

29 For cross-country and country specific evidence, see Criscuolo et al. (2010), see Reference 8; Santos-Paulino AU (2011) Trade specialization, export productivity and growth in Brazil, China, India, South Africa, and a cross section of countries. *Economic Change and Restructuring*, 44(1–2): 75–97; Dachs, B, Ebersberger, B, Kinkel, S et al. (2015) The effects of production offshoring on R&D and innovation in the home country. *Economia e Politica Industriale* 42: 9–31. https://doi.org/10.1007/s40812-014-0001-2

30 For cross-country and country specific evidence, see Criscuolo P, Narula R and Verspagen B (2005) Role of home and host country innovation systems in R&D internationalisation: A patent citation analysis. *Economics of Innovation and New Technology*, 14(5): 417–433; Howells J, Gagliardi D and Malik K (2008) The growth and management of R&D outsourcing: Evidence from UK pharmaceuticals. *R&D Management*, 38(2): 205–219; Jabbour L and Zuniga P (2016) The outsourcing of research and development in global markets: Evidence from France. *World Economy*, 39(3): 339–368.

31 Tapon F and Thong M (1999) Research collaborations by multi-national research oriented pharmaceutical firms: 1988–1997. *R&D Management*, 29(3): 219–231.

32 Bathelt H, Malmberg A and Maskell P (2004) Clusters and knowledge: Local buzz, global pipelines and the process of knowledge creation. *Progress in Human Geography*, 28(1): 31–56. https://doi.org/10.1191%2F0309132504ph469oa

33 Shah I, He L, Hatfield R and Haroon M (2020) *Outward FDI: National and Regional Policy Implications for Technology Innovation* (Working Paper). Department of Economics, University of Bath. https://researchportal.bath.ac.uk/en/publications/outward-fdi-national-and-regional-policy-implications-for-technol

34 Defever, F (2012) The spatial organization of multinational firms. *Canadian Journal of Economics/Revue canadienne d'économique*, 45: 672–697. https://doi.org/10.1111/j.1540-5982.2012.01708.x

35 Defever (2010), see Reference 34.

36 Belderbos R, Sleuwaegen L, Somers D and De Backer K (2016) *Where to Locate Innovative Activities in Global Value Chains*. Paris: OECD. https://doi.org/10.1787/5jlv8zmp86jg-en

37 Crinò (2009), see Reference 28.

38 Propris et al. (2008), see Reference 2.

39 Propris et al. (2008), see Reference 2.

40 Nieto MJ and Rodríguez A (2011) Offshoring of R&D: Looking abroad to improve innovation performance. *Journal of International Business Studies*, 42(3): 345–361.

41 For examples, see Creszenzi, R and Harman O with Arnold D (2018) Move on up! Building, embedding and reshaping global value chains through investment flows: Insights for regional innovation policies. Background paper for an OECD/EC Workshop on 21 September 2018 within the workshop series "Broadening innovation policy: New insights for regions and cities", Paris. https://www.oecd.org/cfe/regionaldevelopment/CrescenziHarman(2018)MoveOnUp.pdf

43   Elliott R, Jabbou L and Vanino E (2018) External knowledge and foreign market access: Evidence from French firms. Paper presented at conference on *Multinationals, Value Chains and Innovation in Regions Around the World*. London: London School of Economics and Political Science (LSE).

44   Crescenzi R, Ganau R and Storper M (2021) Does foreign investment hurt job creation at home? The geography of outward FDI and employment in the USA. *Journal of Economic Geography*, 22(1): 53–79. doi:10.1093/jeg/lbab016.

45   Crescenzi et al. (2021), see Reference 44.

46   Ibarra-Olivo JE (2019) The Economic Geography of Foreign Direct Investment and Human Capital in Mexican Regions. PhD thesis, London School of Economics and Political Science (LSE).

47   Lessard D and Lucea R (2009) Embracing risk as a core competence: The case of CEMEX. *Journal of International Management*, 15(3): 296–305.

48   Basave Kunhardt J (2016) *Multinacionales mexicanas surgimiento y evolución*. Instituto de Investigaciones Económicas, Siglo XXI Editores, S.A. de C.V. http://www.libros.unam.mx/multina-cionales-mexicanas-surgimiento-y-evolucion-9786070282232-libro.html

49   Ekholm K and Hakkala K (2006) The effect of offshoring on labour demand: Evidence from Sweden (Discussion Paper No. 5648, April). London: Centre for Economic Policy Research (CEPR); Hakkala KN, Heyman F and Sjöholm F (2010) Multinationals, skills, and wage elasticities. *Review of World Economics*, 146(2): 263–280.

50   Crescenzi R and Ganau R (2022) *When the Rain Comes, Don't Stay at Home! Regional Innovation and Foreign Investment in the Aftermath of the Great Recession*. Economic Geography and Spatial Economics Series (36). Department of Geography and Environment, London School of Economics and Political Science, London, UK. https://eprints.lse.ac.uk/116878/.

51   Bair J and Gereffi G (2001) Local clusters in global chains: The causes and consequences of export dynamism in Torreon's blue jeans industry. *World Development*, 29(11): 1885–1903. https://doi.org/10.1016/S0305-750X(01)00075-4; Crescenzi R and Iammarino S (2017) Global investments and regional development trajectories: The missing links. *Regional Studies*, 51(1): 97–115. https://doi.org/10.1080/00343404.2016.1262016; De Marchi V, Di Maria E and Gereffi G (2017) *Local Clusters in Global Value Chains: Linking Actors and Territories Through Manufacturing and Innovation*. Abingdon: Routledge.

52   Iammarino S and McCann P (2013) *Multinationals and Economic Geography: Location, Technology and Innovation*. Cheltenham: Edward Elgar.

53   Organisation for Economic Co-operation and Development (OECD) (2016) *OECD Regional Outlook 2016: Productive Regions for Inclusive Societies*. Paris: OECD Publ.

54   Alcácer J and Chung W (2007) Location strategies and knowledge spillovers. *Management Science*, 53(5): 760–776.

55   Crescenzi R, Dyèvre A and Neffke F (2022) Innovation catalysts: How multinationals reshape the global geography of innovation. *Economic Geography*, 98: 199–227. doi:10.1080/00130095.2022.2026766.

56   Konings J (2001) The effects of foreign direct investment on domestic firms: Evidence from firm-level panel data in emerging economies. *Economics of Transition*, 9(3): 619–633.

57 Damijan JP, Knell M, Majcen B and Rojec M (2003) The role of FDI, R&D accumulation and trade in transferring technology to transition countries: Evidence from firm panel data for eight transition countries. *Economic Systems*, 27(2): 189–204.

58 Aghion P, Bloom N, Blundell R, Griffith R and Howitt P (2005) Competition and innovation: An inverted-U relationship. *Quarterly Journal of Economics*, 120(2): 701–728.

59 Rodrik D (2018) *New Technologies, Global Value Chains, and Developing Economies*. Cambridge, MA: National Bureau of Economic Research (NBER).

60 Propris et al. (2008), see Reference 2.

61 Granovetter M (1985) Economic action and social structure: The problem of embeddedness. *American Journal of Sociology*, 91(3): 481–510.

62 Boschma R (2005) Proximity and innovation: A critical assessment. *Regional Studies*, 39(1): 61–74.

63 Propris et al. (2008), see Reference 2.

64 Maskell P and Malmberg A (1999) Localised learning and industrial competitiveness. *Cambridge Journal of Economics*, 23(2): 167–185; Capello R and Faggian A (2005) Collective learning and relational capital in local innovation processes. *Regional Studies*, 39(1): 75–87.

65 Pitelis C (2012) Clusters, entrepreneurial ecosystem co-creation, and appropriability: A conceptual framework. *Industrial and Corporate Change*, 21(6): 1359–1388.

5. How to upgrade through regional policy: reshaping GVCs through FDI

Keywords: leadership; innovation; investment promotion agencies; local content units; institutions; upgrading

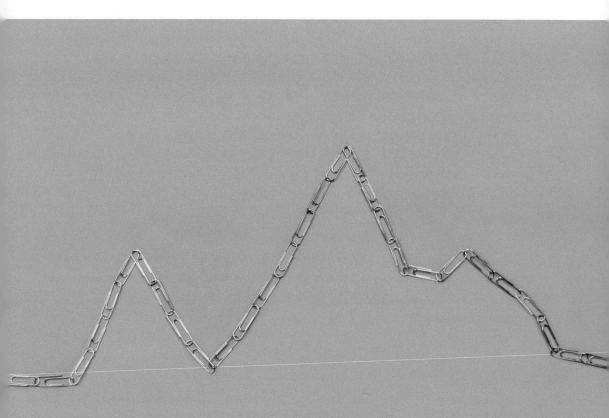

Reshaping GVCs is the process of governments creating the best possible environment to facilitate their firms' insertion into GVCs. To this end, proponents have suggested that this GVC policy agenda is a domestic one.[1] Previous chapters have shown why the region should lead this facilitation. There is increasing adoption of newer targeted industrial policies which, through specific interventions, would see governments managing their FDI inflows and directing them into sectors or tasks of their choice. Such parts of the value chain would be on the receiving end of deliberate targeted promotional efforts,[2] with many such policies being different in character, and thus producing different outcomes than those before.[3] Regional decision-makers can develop specific skills, relevant technologies and markets, and develop partnerships. These will help create investment and provide the opportunity for upgrading investment and innovation.[4] Fortunately, it is understood that when targeting key areas for growth, governments—particularly those in emerging economies—orientate around GVCs.[5] There is a crucial importance for reshaping.

However, alongside designing policies to influence the participation and positioning of local firms, **subnational governments must simultaneously work with other governments at the national and international levels with regards to GVC rules at the systemic level**.[6] It is these agreements that influence the firm's ability to trade and invest within GVCs. Regional decision-makers must ensure that the construction of these agreements account for their requirements.

Regional Studies Policy Impact Books
© 2023 Riccardo Crescenzi and Oliver Harman

https://doi.org/10.1080/2578711X.2022.2099173

Reshaping GVCs, consequently, is an integral part of the discussion on regional economic development and innovation strategies. The broad framing of policy implications is twofold:

1) **Long-term fixed**: fixing the region's operating environment, the rules of the game.
2) **Short-term flexible**: flexible tools allowing the region to interact successfully with variation in the framework.

The policy implications are as follows: firstly as actions for regional leaders, both in regional institutions and international dialogue; secondly as a diagnostic tool to better understand GVCs in a specific region; and thirdly a direct GVC sensitive regional policy to effectively enhance the link between FDI and GVCs.

There is a general requirement for gaining from the benefits of FDI and international technology transfer for the development of host economies. This requirement is for **modern institutional and governance structures as well as conducive innovation systems**. Depending on the stage of the investment, the national and regional levels have different roles to play. Their roles are to consider where MNE subsidiaries will fit into the organisation of a wider GVC.[7] A further leadership role can be played by a region—both regional governments and public agencies can help align industrial policy with structural change.[8]

To understand their ability to capture value, **regional decision-makers need to diagnose where their current competitive advantage is**.[9] This characterises the subnational fine-grained specialisms. This identification and positioning of a region in comparison with its peers is similar to developing a "brand" in a specific place.[10] **The region should strategise in order to position itself successfully, and uniquely from other regions**. However, in doing so, it must also develop itself in a way that—considering the "fragmentation"[11] of value chains—does not leave it stuck in one part. This approach is similar to the entrepreneurial discovery process of Smart Specialisation Strategies (S3)—prioritising investments and public policy based on stakeholder engagement and market dynamics. For GVCs and innovation, **mapping and diagnosis are, therefore, necessary tools**.

When attracting MNEs or lead firms in the GVC to a region, positive spillovers and linkages do not necessarily occur. Technological differences and absorption capabilities, amongst other factors, matter. Therefore, **tools to help invite and provide the right kind of FDI, with the right kind of firm on the other end will enhance the link and the connection with the GVC**.

The process of reshaping and guiding dynamics at a regional level involves recognising and enhancing the key vehicles. It is through these vehicles, which can include FDI and MNEs, that international competitiveness is fostered. Together, in the co-creation of this regional value, the regional government cannot take a passive role, particularly if they want to engage and upgrade these engagements with global markets.[12] The following sections detail why reshaping is necessary and why regions and local decision-makers within them must drive the policy change.

5.1 REGIONAL LEADERSHIP

Regional institutions: in the national framework

Formal and informal institutions generally matter for FDI flows.[13] Consequently, they are also essential factors in shaping and reshaping GVCs through FDI. Evidence shows that institutions can shape the behaviour of MNEs, and the behaviour of MNEs can shape institutions.[14] Therefore, there might be a potential circular role that institutions can play in reshaping GVCs, and vice versa, which deserves careful consideration.

If regional policy decision-makers want to increase the chances of embedding and reshaping GVCs in their regions, then **the capacity of both national and regional institutions is critical**. In the age of GVCs, greater international, national[15] and therefore subnational cooperation is urgent. Knowing this, regional leadership can play a role in delivering and promoting institutional change that works. This change can be implemented by improving the overall business environment of the region and the country, or pushing legislation to improve intellectual property rights. The hope is that regional leadership will act for national benefit. However, this may not be the case, with regions instead acting in their specific interests. Territorial competition as noted in Western Europe in the early 1990s[16] is still seen today in the United States—for example—with Amazon's new headquarters bidding process. The competition can result in MNEs extracting some form of rent through offered incentive packages. Such **targeted subsides are a less successful policy,[17] leading to inefficiently spent public funds and a race to bottom**. More detrimental than this, as is being seen, is that MNEs' feedback might start to dictate regional policy.[18] **A key recommendation for driving productivity is the need for strategic investment instead of subsidies**.[19] This is the vertical policy interacting with GVCs rather than horizontal policy waiting for them to "touch down". It removes geographical local neighbour-fighting-neighbour and replaces it with **global regions leveraging each other's competitive advantage and skills**.

Beyond this territorial competition, some regional leaders are starting from very different institutional contexts.[20] Less developed regions may have very different capacities to those at the frontier. It is, therefore, difficult to determine the roles they can play. Good institutions act as the umbrella for delivering further policy implications, and the emerging picture is one where national institutions may shape GVCs. There is an abundance of evidence on the role of national institutions in attracting MNEs, but less knowledge on regional institutions. A large part of this is due to the conceptualisation and definition of institutions, and a lack of data available at the regional level. This forces measurement of GVCs to be carried out at the national level instead. Measurement aside, **it may be that regional institutions play an even more prominent role in shaping GVCs** when considering that national institutions can be too distant and detached from organisations to effectively influence their behaviour.[21] The actual role that regional institutions play in reshaping GVCs and the behaviour of MNEs

 https://doi.org/10.1080/2578711X.2022.2099173

through the attraction and shaping of FDI is likely to be crucial. For now, the policy implications for reshaping GVCs highlighted should be taken on by those in regional leadership positions—prominent subnational officials working with national authorities.

Regional lobbying: international agreements and embedding GVCs

Recent decades have seen the proliferation of cross-country free trade agreements (FTAs). FTAs can distort sourcing decisions through two channels: lower tariffs when importing from FTA partners and rules of origin (RoO).[22] RoO require sourcing or input of a minimum level of inputs to take place within the free trade area to allow tariff-free export. By distorting sourcing decisions, they are reshaping GVCs. The implementation of the North American Free Trade Agreement's (NAFTA) RoO has led to a considerable reduction in imports of intermediate goods from countries not engaged in the FTA relative to NAFTA partners.[23]

Currently, virtually all lobbying firms support FTAs of some sorts. Larger firms and those engaged with international trade are more likely to lobby in favour of the best possible arrangement given their strategic objectives.[24] Nevertheless, there are various implications of this. Having entered FTAs, small and medium-sized enterprises (SMEs) may find it too costly to comply with RoO. Furthermore, larger MNEs may have to reshape their global value chains if they want to continue exporting duty free. Given the within-country variation in the location of firms of different sizes and active in different sectors, the implications of different types of agreements affect subnational units in various ways. **The GVC impact is not felt equally**.

Although the perception is that this is a macro-phenomenon, there is a subnational role to play. **Regions have the potential to work together in interregional networks to reshape GVCs**. By forming regional groups with similar interests, they should be able to influence the shaping of macro-GVC agreements and alter the GVC framework to account for their differences. Potential gains could arise for them by lobbying and ensuring that FTAs bring benefits to their value chains. Regional development policy needs to reflect regional needs, including the understanding of how any international FTA would affect their regional firms. Considering how GVCs have led to increasingly fragmented and dispersed production processes across countries, it is no longer as easy as "free trade wins over all". **Regions have specific, place-based advantages that may be ignored by international agreements that do not account for this**. They need to ensure the broader long-term fixed trade framework they work within is set to their advantage and coordinated with their active regional policies. To make this case, regional leaders need:

- **To be able to cooperate with other regions** addressing coordination failure problems that jeopardise many bottom-up policies. Together, they can make it necessary for the national government to act as a facilitator (e.g., the case of interregional infrastructure).

- **To develop competencies and administrative capabilities** to elaborate a consistent strategy reflecting the genuine demands of local actors. This capacity is often lacking in less developed regions, generating a potentially vicious circle.

- **To be cognisant of their place** (and that of their firms) in GVCs. This assessment is where GVC mapping comes in.

Regional certification: accreditation on the GVC stage

Firms may initially build GVCs to exploit vertical integration of suppliers for production benefits, but this does not restrict upgrading. The **certification of regional firm practices and adoption of standards on a global stage can change outputs in a GVC**. This change can occur at developing level where, for example, certification on quality in Mali's cotton sector supported the reshaping and upgrading in GVCs by the firms.[25] In just three years, the quality and subsequent value doubled. Similarly, a strong standards regime helped Pakistan to overcome a ban on fish—particularly important for export and livelihoods in the Sindh region.[26] Using technological standards as another example, it is estimated they directly effect at least 80% of international trade,[27] and are unavoidable to a large extent in manufacturing or services.

A key example in this regard is the geographical indications (GIs) granted by the European Union (EU) to recognise and certify products associated with a specific region of origin and with traditional production techniques that can offer tangible opportunities for local economic development in rural areas. **By signalling to global markets and protecting unique agri-food products from unfair competition, GIs offer rural economies the opportunity to link up with global markets while retaining their uniqueness**.

The most renowned agri-food product that has benefitted from Protected Designation of Origin (PDO) or Protected Geographical Indications (PGI) is wine. Rural areas whose wine production is protected by a GI experience lower population decline and a reorganisation of the economy towards higher value-added activities (non-farming versus farming sectors) compared with other rural areas which have similar characteristics but are unable to rely on the protection and recognition offered by GIs.[28] In other words, with limited budget resources, the EU has been able to provide its rural areas the opportunity to become part of, and benefit from, global economic integration and trade flows precisely by being (and remaining) local. GIs establish new global–local linkages that also foster participation in GVCs and upgrading. The product–region of origin is exploited for the differentiation of the product that becomes unique and distinct from the majority of other agri-food goods. Those goods, on the contrary, are produced in a context of increasing standardisation and homogeneity.

The certification does not have to be driven by subnational government; increasingly applying recognised standards across GVCs is led by lead firms. Regions should collaborate with these lead firms to enhance the quality and value-added of their product or service.

 https://doi.org/10.1080/2578711X.2022.2099173

5.2 A DIAGNOSTIC TOOL: GVC MAPPING AND ANALYSIS

The typical useful approach to understanding particular GVCs is mapping and analysis.[29] That is:

> For regions to develop a value capture strategy, they first need to diagnose their extant and evolving comparative and competitive advantages. This strategy involves deciding whether to "compete" on their existing strengths or to develop new advantages in new specialisms.[30]

Value chain analysis and mapping is a diagnostic tool for understanding potential economic trajectories. The method seeks to clarify in which geography and with which activities the stakeholders involved in the chain engage, whether it is those who are taking a good or service from its initial stages of production, or those at later stages who take it onwards to the consumer. Mapping is important as a stock-take for current tasks and skills base, as well as for anticipated change and economic transition.[31] Such value chain analysis can also look to establish dynamic factors such as the governance or interfirm relationships that influence the locally produced product or service. Together, they provide the baseline for making informed decisions on how GVC actors can build, embed or reshape their actions along the chain by understanding both regional and firm preferences.

Case study 5: Removing upgrading bottlenecks in Emilia-Romagna, Italy, and Antigua, Guatemala

In 2015 the region of Emilia-Romagna in Italy[32] mapped the knowledge and competencies available, allowing the identification of 27 GVCs in five primary sectors. The region could then pursue certain activities effectively. The mapping exercise allowed all regional actors of the GVCs to meet and interact, define common goals, and critically work towards reshaping GVCs. Emilia-Romagna strengthened its territorial identity, building a globally acknowledged local advantage. Mapping can also be useful for identifying regional bottlenecks. This use occurred in the tourism service sector in Antigua, Guatemala. Here, with links analysed, regional tourism stakeholders could facilitate and coordinate industrial policy to overcome the bottlenecks, strengthening the chain and allowing for economic and social upgrading.[33] "Systemic" bottlenecks such as institutional incentives for investment, as well as "link" bottlenecks such as lack of municipal or intermunicipal tourism enterprises inhibited tourism development. The Regional Department of Sacatepéquez, the region surrounding Antigua city, consequently developed an action-orientated value chain-strengthening strategy to remove these bottlenecks

---

Data and mapping to develop research and policy for the new paradigm

In addition to understanding and mapping the links between the chain, it is important to understand their empirical basis. Here, the development of input–output tables allowed the development of the new paradigm. These empirics underpinned[34] the conceptualisation of the production process in terms of component tasks with data. However, measures based on these indicators remain completely aspatial, making it difficult to offer insights for local policymakers. A turning point for quantitative analyses capable of informing regional development policies is constituted by the availability of firm-level datasets. These datasets contain information on the import and export transactions of firms that make it possible to compute indexes of GVC participation in line with those based on global input–output tables. Transaction-level customs datasets (such as the Export Dynamics Database by the World Bank) make it possible to identify firms that are active in international trade by importing and/or exporting. Participation in GVCs is approximated by the simultaneous engagement in both import and export activities by the same firm. More comprehensive information at the product level would make it possible to further qualify firm-level participation in GVCs by distinguishing firms that do import intermediate goods (to be used as inputs for their own exports) from imports of final goods. The integration of custom data across countries would allow one to further track the products of the focal firms into the destination country, capturing the various GVC stages in full.

Where the geolocation of firms or establishments is possible, this type of firm-level dataset paves the way for a complete understanding of regional GVC participation. Furthermore, the understanding will crucially engage with impacts in terms of labour markets, productivity, inequalities and innovation. An interesting practical example of analyses that leverage firm-level data that could potentially be extended for regional-level studies is offered by seminal work[35] that combines input–output data with detailed establishment-level data. The work analyses firms' propensity to integrate up- versus downstream inputs in more than 100 countries. The study captures the variation of GVC linkages across firms, thus allowing for a finer understanding of firms' input sourcing decisions, the way import and export participation are linked, and how MNEs organise their production networks.[36]

The more extensive use of firm-level data offers the possibility to develop more sophisticated and nuanced analyses of GVCs. This can be achieved by establishing the links between firms in different countries and at different stages of the production process.[37] These links can create the conditions to **bridge the case study approach to the analysis and mapping of GVCs[38] to that of quantitative work on GVCs covering multiple sectors, regions and countries simultaneously**.[39] The geolocalisation of these datasets and their integration in regional statistics will offer the possibility of further bridging these two streams of research.

Further work is needed in order to extend the bridging between case studies and the quantitative analysis of GVCs. With this bridge, policy decision-makers will be able to embrace a geospatial approach needed to inform regional policies aimed at building, embedding and reshaping GVCs.

5.3 A REGIONAL POLICY: INVESTMENT PROMOTION AGENCIES AND LOCAL CONTENT UNITS

Reshaping and promoting GVCs through FDI and harnessing measures intended to promote competitive internationalisation is not a generally appreciated or accepted view.[40] Unfortunately, ambiguity remains about whether participating in GVCs is even a policy worth pursuing, since development benefits are sometimes difficult to derive.[41] As a result, and as outlined above, an active policy where governments proactively address the bottlenecks and market failures preventing FDI inflows into areas of their choice is finding a favourable response.[42]

Investment promotion agencies (IPAs)

One mechanism through which regional policies can shape GVCs is by influencing the behaviour of MNEs and their foreign investment decisions. These policies account for aforementioned firm and location variation. A prominent example of these types of policies is the establishment of IPAs—one of the most widespread initiatives to attract FDI.[43] IPAs predominantly look at inward investment and are conceptually justified on the basis that transaction costs, imperfect information and information asymmetries are present when investing, and there is thus a fundamental market failure which IPAs can help overcome.[44] With IPAs, MNE investment choices are better matched with regions and their self discovered comparative advantages. IPAs interact with the variation at the firm level and how this affects FDI, thereby ensuring opportune regional GVC-building. This interaction mitigates the considerable informational disadvantages that foreign investors experience as opposed to domestic investors.[45] **By attracting FDI, IPAs can help reshape GVCs as firms and their activities enter regions.**

Not only are they conceptually justified, but empirically justified too. Looking at evidence from IPAs in 124 countries, **at the national level, sectors designated as a priority for investment promotion received more than twice as much FDI as non-priority sectors**.[46] Well-planned IPAs and strategies were critical in attracting transformative GVC investments by MNEs in Costa Rica, Malaysia and Morocco, where both building and embedding GVC through FDI required well-formulated investment policy.[47] The IPAs allowed a boost in comparative advantage through fine-grained specialism.[48] Currently, the grouping of investment promotion functions and mandates can be divided into five categories:

- National image-building.

- Investment generation.

- Investor servicing.

- Policy advocacy.

- Investment aftercare.

The final element is particularly useful to consider. Aftercare looks at the corporate evolution of MNEs, how to reshape the GVC, and upgrade through it in the long-term.[49]

IPAs represent a cost-efficient way of attracting the right kind of FDI. Recent evidence found that every US$1 on investment promotion led to almost US$200 in FDI inflow, resulting in each new job in investment-promoted sectors costing less than US$80.[50] For this they need clear objectives in the fixed framework of broader economic development strategies, as well as effective design and management. The IPA reduces information costs and subsequent cognitive distance. In doing so, it can in principle help build the preconditions for the first link with the GVC. Thus, **IPAs can play a crucial role in influencing FDI decisions and reducing entry costs.** This is by enhancing their knowledge of local fundamentals.[51] However, while the evidence offers some support for IPAs as a tool to build GVCs through FDI, the capacity to embed them into the domestic economy to generate transformation and upgrading remains conditional. This condition is the design of complementary measures going beyond investment promotion. In order to avoid "cathedrals in the desert" scenarios where foreign activities remain isolated from the host economy, three key considerations are of particular importance:

- The action of IPAs cannot stop with the announcement of the investment. **Aftercare and continued support for the operations of the foreign investor are of paramount importance**, but are often overlooked.

- **Investment attraction should be coupled and coordinated with other tools designed to embed different activities** into the domestic economy. Foreign firms face higher opportunity-cost in engaging in collaborative projects with domestic firms even when public subsidies are made available.

- IPAs often target foreign investors with a sectoral logic based on the identification of a set of priority sectors. However, as discussed in chapter 2, **upgrading requires the adoption of a different approach focused on functions and tasks in a GVC logic**—an approach that is still not common in these organisations.

IPAs are also a potential policy tool for lagging regions, and **regional IPAs have indeed become increasingly common in both advanced and emerging economies**. These subnational organisations work—with various degrees of coordination and complementarity—together with their national counterparts for the attraction of FDI. They might even work better than their national counterparts since they are in closer proximity to in regions-sectors targeted by sub-national IPAs investor's operations.[52] They have a critical role to play in making better use of limited fiscal resources and managing related investment.[53] Recent evidence looks at the impact of national and regional IPA targeting specific key sectors and not others.[54] Results show an increase of almost 25% in FDI and a similar jump in FDI-related jobs[55]—**regionally targeted sectors see increases in FDI.** While national IPAs may shift or coordinate FDI, subnational IPAs are more generative in change. This evidence seems to be true in both advanced and less developed EU regions. In less developed areas where market and institutional failures are stronger, the subnational IPAs work better, potentially driving improvements in business environment. Therefore, IPAs seem to have an important role to play, specifically in giving priority to attracting investors and removing any restrictions to value chain formation.

Case study 6: Subnational IPAs, North Middle Sweden

IPAs are increasingly used as a policy tool with more nations and regions registering them.[56] Current evidence points to regional IPAs working—bringing in foreign companies, investment and local jobs. The local targeting towards specific key sectors and tasks in the local economy sees regional IPAs' impact being more tangible than that of national IPAs. At a national level, agencies may just redistribute global investment flows rather than increase them.[57]

Regional IPAs of particular note are in Sweden, where they score highly on their quality.[58] From a policy perspective, if resource-scarce policy decision-makers wish to establish regional IPAs, the most gains are achievable in less developed areas of their country. This is because they have a greater chance to remove or by-pass investors' operational bottlenecks, poor information provision or low-capacity institutions. Subnational IPAs in these regions can compensate for these poor foundations where active engagement with investors makes up for passive subnational inadequacies.[59] Regional IPAs act as the interface between foreign investors and local investment ecosystems that, as a result, become more transparent and receptive, notwithstanding the generally lower quality of local government in less advanced regions. Indeed, regional IPAs can contribute to the improvement of local quality of government by collecting input from investors and scanning international best practices to be adapted and transferred to the benefit of the region. This benefit is particularly true in knowledge-intensive sectors where collaboration is key to success.[60] Therefore, their role in upgrading is crucial. Sweden exemplifies this, with the North Middle region having the lowest human development indicators. Partially to counter this, each county has its own regional IPA. This is Invest in Dalarna, Invest in Gävlebord and Business Värmland, with investor services focus on steel, forestry and advanced engineering as examples

---

Regional policy decision-makers should look at implementing IPAs, but only once they have undertaken a GVC mapping exercise. **It is critical to identify where the region will build, embed and reshape.** FDI flows, both inward and outward if used correctly, can bring positive effects to a policy decision-maker's region. **The promotion of outward investments (also through IPAs) is another useful tool. IPAs have successfully assisted domestic and foreign companies investing abroad for years.**[61] This assistance can take shape in a variety of forms, from the analyses of country and product trends to technical assistance, support and co-financing which take advantage of such trends. The support for active internationalisation of domestic firms fits nicely with the evidence showing knowledge benefits to the home region of firms that offshore abroad. Although less is known empirically, programmes to promote and service investment abroad can be beneficial to the regional economy and its GVC positioning. The private sector also has a role to play in collaborating with IPAs to carry out joint promotional activities.[62] Together, they can bring back those sources of knowledge via their network connections.[63]

Local content and linkage units and enterprise mapping

While the IPA may bring in general FDI, local content or local linkage units (LCU) are different. **LCUs are bodies set up within or alongside investment promotion departments that enable new connections between investors (FDI) and suppliers (SME/MNE local linkages). LCUs are described as a matchmaking service.**[64] They can interact with the differences at the regional level and how this affects the FDI outflow. In doing so, they ensure opportune regional GVC embedding. It is the LCU that can piggyback on MNEs and try to get local companies integrated into their supply chains.[65]

To best harness the benefits of FDI, attention should be placed on enhancing the potential for spillovers. This potential is mainly through backward linkages—inputs into exports.[66] The evidence of FDI spillovers shows that the main benefits flow through the vertical linkages of MNEs, particularly direct technical assistance from lead firms. This can be through formal linkage programmes or more informal functioning relationships—assistance which creates one of the largest spillovers to local SMEs.[67]

This evidence base encourages the creation of LCUs. The LCU can allow dialogue and engagement with the MNE to arrive at the best local firm involved in the value chain. **Often working better than strict local content legislation, LCUs are flexible and form a relationship-building approach.** Here, engagement is better than prescription. The stricter requirements may distort the decision-making process, restricting investment. This occurred in Brazil with the poor experience of promoting local suppliers in the automotive sector. Again, proactive policy engagement works, where active engagement with MNEs is evidenced as a tried and trusted international formula for using local companies in the value chain.[68] The linkage itself need not be content based. Direct technical assistance from lead firms is one of the biggest sources of spillovers to local suppliers.[69] At a regional level, LCUs are less prevalent; however, at a national level, success has been seen.

https://doi.org/10.1080/2578711X.2022.2099173

Case study 7: Linkages programmes in Ireland and Singapore

Both Ireland and Singapore can highlight specific examples at a national level. The Irish National Linkages Programme had two key components. One was working on accounting for firm differences and the other SME upgrading. Through targeting both MNEs and local firms, the programme both found links and helped build capacity. This targeting process also looked at SMEs and their ability to improve or upgrade their capabilities.[70] The successful programme has now evolved into a more comprehensive initiative working at incorporating Irish companies into GVCs.

Singapore used a Local Industry Upgrading Programme. Here, upgrading occurred through the training of local firms, but perhaps uniquely this responsibility fell to the MNE. The MNE would second an employee to the local SME allowing direct knowledge transfer, and in return the Upgrading Programme paid the employee's salary—a leasing of staff. Both these examples focus on capacity and upgrading, and can thus be useful to both technological frontier and lagging regions. In conjunction with private-firm linkages, public–academic linkages driven by LCUs can be of benefit. Embedding MNEs in local university structures should lead to further knowledge transfer. The incorporation of cutting-edge thinking, university start-ups and accelerators should see two-way benefits, at the MNE and regional levels

Enterprise mapping meanwhile is the systematic and comprehensive account of the industrial sectors. It has, for example, been completed in Mozambique.[71] **It helps remove information asymmetries through detailed profiles of leading firms**. Location and firm can be matched, and enterprise maps can be useful for coercing global investment flows as well as for policy decision-makers who wish to foster upgrading and industrial development. Combined with enterprise mapping, investment promotion agencies (IPAs) are complementary and useful policy tools. For enterprise mapping aims to provide a detailed profile of both the industries and leading companies in the area of economic study, which the IPAs can leverage. Again, the removal of cognitive distance and restrictions can lead to value chain formation.

Case study 8: Firm mapping in Costa Rica

Although not at a subnational level, useful mapping has also taken place at the firm level in Costa Rica. Costa Rica Provee (CRP) addressed the market failures associated with information problems[72] by operating a business matchmaking service. A critical first step in dealing with the uniqueness across firms was to map SME capabilities. By focusing on SMEs with enhanced capabilities—and therefore a higher likelihood of becoming successful linkages to multinational corporations—between 2001 and 2012 the programme created 1355 linkages between over 400 local companies and over 300 predominantly MNE exporters.[73] Assisted firms still see benefits today, from knowledge transfers as a result of these MNE relationships.[74] Although an effective matchmaking mechanism,[75] over 80% of the linkages lacked incorporation into MNEs' final high-technology products. SME firm input, unfortunately, remained broadly non-specialised with only some upgrading taking place

More broadly in Costa Rica, domestic firms that started supplying MNEs experienced strong and lasting gains in firm performance. Becoming a supplier to an MNE can be transformative: four years after connection, firms experienced over 25% more staff hired, almost 10% higher profits per worker, and between 5% and 10% productivity gain

Figure 5.1   Role of IPAs and LCUs in generating impact from GVC investment

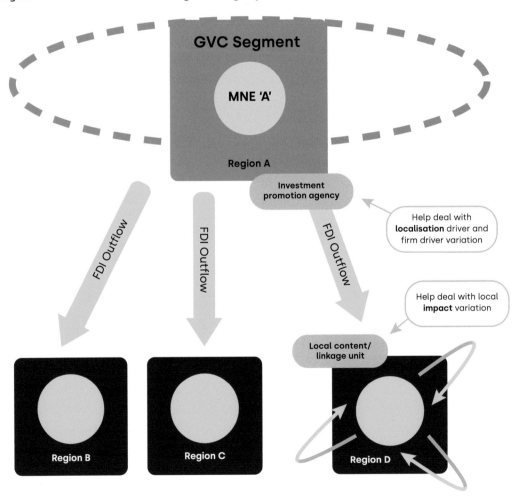

Source: Authors' elaboration

https://doi.org/10.1080/2578711X.2022.2099173

In sum, IPAs and the process of GVC upgrading work well together. By concentrating in sectors and in particular tasks where their areas of influence have a comparative advantage, sectors can allow diversification, bringing advanced technologies and skills to their host economies.[76] When thinking about IPAs, there is a trade-off between more intensive coordinated specialised support and less specialised, centralised, easier-to-implement organisations.[77] However, targeting is necessary in allowing messages to be tailored and focused. Emphasising efforts to a particular audience can help deal with both locational and firm applicability, increasing effectiveness.[78] **This targeting must go past exclusively matchmaking.** As was seen in Costa Rica, additional support is necessary to upgrade these targeted linkages into higher value-added goods and services.[79]

Reshaping GVCs is therefore as much as about the correct mapping and promotion as it is the characteristics of the local innovation and support system.[80] Regional policy decision-makers, therefore, have many tools at their disposal to reshape GVCs in their areas. It is those tools that account for the firm and locational variance and which stand the most chance of success. Figure 5.1 demonstrates this. **There is, however, a necessary coordination of tools.** For example, if a trade framework does not correlate with what IPAs are hoping to deliver, then it would stifle their ability to bring benefit to the region. These trade frameworks are the policy networks regions must work within. Therefore, **alignment is key between global policy negotiations and regional delivery**.

NOTES

1 Stephenson S and Pfister A-K (2017) Who governs global value chains? In D Elms, A Hassani, A and P Low (eds.), *The Intangible Economy: How Services Shape Global Production and Consumption*, pp. 55–81. Cambridge, UK: Cambridge University Press. https://doi.org/10.1017/9781108235938.005

2 Draper P and Freytag A (2014) *Who Captures the Value in Global Value Chains? High Level Implications for the World Trade Organisation*. The E15 Initiative, International Centre for Trade and Sustainable Development & World Economic Forum. http://e15initiative.org/publications/who-captures-the-value-in-the-global-value-chain-high-level-implications-for-the-world-trade-organization/

3 Gereffi G (2019) Global value chains, development, and emerging economies. In P Lund-Thomsen, M Wendelboe Hansen and A Lindgreen (eds.), *Business and Development Studies: Issues and Perspectives*, pp. 125–158. Abingdon, UK: Routledge. https://doi.org/10.1017/9781108559423.013

4 Singh H (2014) *Reinvigorating Manufacturing through Industrial Policy and the WTO. E15 Initiative*. E15 Expert Group on Reinvigorating Industrial Policy, Geneva, ICTSD and World Economic Forum (WEF).

5 Gereffi (2019), see Reference 3.

6 Stephenson and Pfister (2017), see Reference 1.

7 Rugman A, Verbeke A and Yuan W (2011) Re-conceptualizing Bartlett and Ghoshal's classification of national subsidiary roles in the multinational enterprise. *Journal of Management Studies*, 48(2): 253–277.

8   Lee K and Malerba F (2017) Catch-up cycles and changes in industrial leadership: Windows of opportunity and responses of firms and countries in the evolution of sectoral systems. *Research Policy*, 46(2): 338–351.

9   Bailey D, Pitelis C and Tomlinson PR (2018) A place-based developmental regional industrial strategy for sustainable capture of co-created value. *Cambridge Journal of Economics*, 42(6): 1521–1542. https://doi.org/10.1093/cje/bey019

10 Konzelmann S, Fovargue-Davies M and Wilkinson F (2018) Britain's industrial evolution: The structuring role of economic theory. *Journal of Economic Issues*, 52(1): 1–30.

11 Venables AJ (1999) Fragmentation and multinational production. *European Economic Review*, 43(4–6): 935–945. https://doi.org/10.1016/S0014-2921(98)00106-8

12 Neilson J, Pritchard B and Yeung HWC (2014) Global value chains and global production networks in the changing international political economy: An introduction. *Review of International Political Economy*, 21(1): 1–8; Bailey et al. (2018), see Reference 9.

13 World Bank Group (2017) *Global Investment Competitiveness Report 2017/2018: Foreign Investor Perspectives and Policy Implications*. Washington, DC: World Bank Group.

14 Cantwell J, Dunning JH and Lundan SM (2010) An evolutionary approach to understanding international business activity: The co-evolution of MNEs and the institutional environment. *Journal of International Business Studies*, 41(4): 567–586.

15 World Bank (2020) World development report 2020: Trading for development in the age of global value chains. In *World Development Report: Trading for Development in the Age of Global Value Chains*. Washington, DC: World Bank. https://www.worldbank.org/en/publication/wdr2020

16 Gordon IR and Jayet H (1994) *Territorial Policies between Cooperation and Competition*. Lille: USTL Université des sciences et technologies de Lille, Faculté des sciences; Cheshire PC and Gordon IR (1996) Territorial competition and the predictability of collective (in) action. *International Journal of Urban and Regional Research*, 20(3): 383–399.

17 Crescenzi R, de Blasio G and Giua M (2020) Cohesion Policy incentives for collaborative industrial research: Evaluation of a Smart Specialisation forerunner programme. *Regional Studies*, 54(10): 1341–1353. doi:10.1080/00343404.2018.1502422.

18 Garfield L (2018, June 3) Amazon's HQ2 competition is pushing 'loser' cities to become the next Silicon Valley—But some experts say it's a dangerous plan. *UK Business Insider*. https://www.businessinsider.in/Amazons-HQ2-competition-is-pushing-loser-cities-to-become-the-next-Silicon-Valley-but-some-experts-say-its-a-dangerous-plan/articleshow/64439157.cms

19 Organisation for Economic Co-operation and Development (OECD) (2016) *OECD Regional Outlook 2016: Productive Regions for Inclusive Societies*. Paris: OECD Publ.

20 Rodríguez-Pose A (2013) Do institutions matter for regional development? *Regional Studies*, 47(7): 1034–1047.

21 Rodríguez-Pose A (1999) Innovation prone and innovation averse societies: Economic performance in Europe. *Growth and Change*, 30(1): 75–105; Rodríguez-Pose (2013), see Reference 20.

22 Conconi P, Sapir A and Zanardi M (2016) The internationalization process of firms: From exports to FDI. *Journal of International Economics* 99: 16–30. https://doi.org/10.1016/j.jinteco.2015.12.004

23 Conconi et al. (2016), see Reference 22.

24 Blanga-Gubbay M, Conconi P and Parenti M (2018) *Globalization for Sale*. CESifo Working Paper No. 8239. https://ssrn.com/abstract=3584090 or http://dx.doi.org/10.2139/ssrn.3584090

25 Auriol E, Balineau GL and Bonneton N (Forthcoming 2022) *The Economics of Quality in Developing Countries*.

26 World Bank (2020), see Reference 15.

27 Purcell D and Kushnier G (2016) Globalization and standardization. *Standards Engineering, The Journal of SES – The Society for Standards Professionals*, March/April.

28 Crescenzi R, De Filippis F, Giua M and Vaquero-Piñeiro C (2022) Geographical indications and local development: The strength of territorial embeddedness. *Regional Studies*, 56(3): 381–393. doi:10.1080/00343404.2021.1946499.

29 Backer KD and Miroudot S (2013) *Mapping Global Value Chains* (Trade Policy Papers No. 159), p. 46. Paris: OECD Publ.; Frederick S (2016) *GVCs Concepts & Tools*. Durham, NC: Duke University. https://gvcc.duke.edu; Gereffi G and Fernandez-Stark K (2016) *Global Value Chain Analysis: A Primer*. Duke University. http://hdl.handle.net/10161/12488.

30 Bailey et al. (2018), see Reference 9, at p. 1531.

31 OECD (2019) *Regions in Industrial Transition: Policies for People and Places*. Paris: OECD Publ.

32 Bianchi P and Labory S (2018) What policies, initiatives or programmes can support attracting, embedding and reshaping GVCs in regions? In *OECD Seminar Series in Broadening Innovation Policy: New Insights for Regions and Cities*. Paris: OECD Publ. https://www.oecd.org/cfe/regionaldevelopment/BianchiLabory(2018)BuildingEmbeddingAndReshapingGlobalValueChains-V2.pdf

33 Oddone N and Alarcón A (2016) *Fortalecimiento de la cadena du Turismo de Antigua Guatemala y do los municipios rurales del departamento de Sacatepéquez, Guatemala*. Mexico City: United Nations Economic Commission for Latin America and the Caribbean (UN-EXLAC) and International Fund for Agricultural Development (IFAD); Perez R and Oddone N (2016) *Strengthening Value Chains: A Toolkit*. UN-ECLAC-IFAD.

34 Grossman GM and Rossi-Hansberg E (2006) The rise of offshoring: It's not wine for cloth anymore. In *The New Economic Geography: Effects and Policy Implications: Proceedings of Jackson Hole Economic Policy Symposium*, pp. 59–102. Kansas City, MO: Federal Reserve Bank of Kansas City.

35 Alfaro L, Antràs P, Chor D and Conconi P (2019) Internalizing global value chains: A firm-level analysis. *Journal of Political Economy*, 127(2): 508–559. doi:10.1086/700935.

36 World Bank and World Trade Organization (WTO) (2019) *Global Value Chain Development Report 2019: Technological Innovation, Supply Chain Trade, and Workers in a Globalized World*. Washington, DC: World Bank Group.

37 For a guide to empirical work, see Ahmad N, Bohn T, Mulder N, Vaillant M and Zaclicever D (2017) *Indicators on Global Value Chains: A Guide for Empirical Work* (Statistics Working Papers No. 2017/08). Paris: OECD Publ. https://doi.org/10.1787/8502992f-en.

38 See much of the seminal work by Gary Gereffi and co-authors, referenced throughout the book, and consolidated in Gereffi G (2018) *Global Value Chains and Development: Redefining the Contours of 21st Century Capitalism*. Cambridge: Cambridge University Press. https://doi.org/10.1017/9781108559423

39 See the work by Pol Antras and Paola Conconi and others, e.g., Alfaro et al. (2019), see Reference 35.

40 Stephenson and Pfister (2017), see Reference 1.

41 Draper and Freytag (2014), see Reference 2.

42 Stiglitz JE, Lin JY and Monga C (2013) Introduction: The rejuvenation of industrial policy. In JE Stiglitz and JY Lin (eds.), *The Industrial Policy Revolution I: The Role of Government Beyond Ideology*, pp. 1–15. London: Palgrave Macmillan.

43 Charlton A and Davis N (2007) Does investment promotion work? *BE Journal of Economic Analysis & Policy*, 7(1). https://doi.org/10.2202/1935-1682.1743; Harding T and Javorcik BS (2011) Roll out the red carpet and they will come: Investment promotion and FDI inflows. *The Economic Journal*, 121(557): 1445–1476. https://doi.org/10.1111/j.1468-0297.2011.02454.x

44 World Bank (2020) *Foreign Direct Investment as a Key Driver for Global Value Chains*. Washington, DC: World Bank, World Bank.

45 Mariotti S and Piscitello L (1995) Information costs and location of FDIs within the host country: Empirical evidence from Italy. *Journal of International Business Studies*, 26(4): 815–841.

46 Harding and Javorcik (2011), see Reference 52.

47 World Bank (2020), see Reference 15.

48 Freund C and Moran T (2017) *Multinational Investors as Export Superstars: How Emerging-Market Governments Can Reshape Comparative Advantage* (Working Paper No. 17-1). Washington DC: Peterson Institute for International Economics. https://dx.doi.org/10.2139/ssrn.2901148

49 United Nations Conference on Trade and Development (UNCTAD) (2007) *World Investment Report 2007: Transnational Corporations, Extractive Industries and Development*. https://worldinvestmentreport.unctad.org/wir2007/; Harding and Javorcik (2011), see Reference 52.

50 Harding and Javorcik (2011), see Reference 52.

51 Loewendahl H (2001) A framework for FDI promotion. *Transnational Corporations*, 10(1): 1–42.; Lim H (2008) *SMEs in Asia and Globalisation*. Jakarta: Economic Research Institute for ASEAN and East Asia. https://www.eria.org/RPR-2007-5.pdf

52 Crescenzi R, Di Cataldo M and Giua M (2021) FDI inflows in Europe: Does investment promotion work? *Journal of International Economics*, 132: 103497. https://doi.org/10.1016/j.jinteco.2021.103497.

53 OECD (2011) *OECD Regional Outlook 2011: Building Resilient Regions for Stronger Economies*. Paris: OECD Publ.

54 Harding and Javorcik (2011), see Reference 52.

55 Crescenzi et al. (2021), see Reference 61.

56 World Association of Investment Promotion Agencies (WAIPA) (2020) *Members of World Association of Investment Promotion Agencies*. https://waipa.org/members/

57 Crescenzi et al. (2021), see Reference 61.

58 Harding and Javorcik (2011), see Reference 52.

59 Crescenzi R, Di Cataldo M and Giua (2021) FDI inflows in Europe: Does investment promotion work? *Journal of International Economics*, 132: 103497. https://doi.org/10.1016/j.jinteco.2021.103497.

60 Crescenzi et al. (2021), see Reference 68.

61   UNCTAD (2015) *Outward Investment Agencies: Industry Global Value Chains, Connectivity and Regional Smart Specialisation in Europe.*

62   Jordana J, Volpe Martincus C and Gallo A (2010) *Export Promotion Organizations in Latin America and the Caribbean: An Institutional Portrait* (Working Paper Series). Inter-American Development Bank. https://publications.iadb.org/publications/english/document/Export-Promotion-Organizations-in-Latin-America-and-the-Caribbean-An-Institutional-Portrait.pdf

63   UNCTAD (2015), see Reference 70.

64   Steenbergen V and Sutton J (2017) *Establishing a Local Content Unit for Rwanda* (Policy Note, Technical Report). London: International Growth Centre. https://www.theigc.org/publication/establishing-local-content-unit-rwanda/

65   Sutton J (2016) *How to Reform an Investment Agency: A Case Study in Organisational Change.* London: International Growth Centre. https://www.youtube.com/watch?v=wDNOW3dOKcE.

66   Sutton J, Jinhage A, Leape J, Newfarmer R and Page J (2016) *Harnessing FDI for Job Creation and Industrialisation in Africa* (Growth Brief No. 27). London: International Growth Centre. https://www.theigc.org/reader/harnessing-fdi-for-job-creation-and-industrialisation-in-africa/

67   Farole T and Winkler D (2014) *Making Foreign Direct Investment Work for Sub-Saharan Africa: Local Spillovers and Competitiveness in Global Value Chains.* Washington, DC: World Bank.

68   Sutton et al. (2016), see Reference 75.

69   Farole and Winkler (2014), see Reference 76.

70   Crespi G, Fernández-Arias E and Stein E (2014) A world of possibilities: Internationalization for productive development. In G Crespi, E Fernández-Arias and E Stein (eds.), *Rethinking Productive Development*, pp. 233–278. Berlin: Springer.

71   Sutton J (2014) *An Enterprise Map of Mozambique.* London: International Growth Centre in association with the London Publishing Partnership.

72   Monge-González R, Rivera L and Rosales-Tijerino J (2010) *Productive Development Policies in Costa Rica: Market Failures, Government Failures, and Policy Outcomes.* Washington DC: Inter-American Development Bank.

73   Crespi et al. (2014), see Reference 79.

74   Monge-González R and Rodriguez-Alvarez J (2013) *Impact Evaluation of Innovation and Linkage Development Programs in Costa Rica: The Cases of Propyme and CR Provee.* Washington DC: Inter-American Development Bank.

75   Paus EA and Gallagher KP (2008) Missing links: Foreign investment and industrial development in Costa Rica and Mexico. *Studies in Comparative International Development*, 43(1): 53–80; Monge-González et al. (2010), see Reference 81.

76   Alfaro L and Charlton A (2007) *Growth and the Quality of Foreign Direct Investment: Is All FDI Equal?* (Discussion Paper No. 830). London: Centre for Economic Performance.

77   Loewendahl (2001), see Reference 60; Economic Commission for Latin America and the Caribbean (ECLAC) (2008) *Structural Change and Productivity Growth, 20 Years Later. Old Problems, New Opportunities.* 32nd sesssion of ECLAC, Santo Domingo, Dominican Republic, 9–13 June 2008.

https://repositorio.cepal.org/handle/11362/2890; Proksch M (2004) Selected issues on promotion and attraction of foreign direct investment in least developed countries and economies in transition. *Investment Promotion and Enterprise Development Bulletin for Asia and the Pacific*, 2: 1–17.

78 Loewendahl (2001), see Reference 60.

79 Crespi et al. (2014), see Reference 79.

80 Morrison A, Pietrobelli C and Rabellotti R (2008) Global value chains and technological capabilities: A framework to study learning and innovation in developing countries. *Oxford Development Studies*, 36(1): 39–58. https://doi.org/10.1080/13600810701848144; Pietrobelli C and Rabellotti R (2011) Global value chains meet innovation systems: Are there learning opportunities for developing countries? *World Development*, 39(7): 1261–1269. https://doi.org/10.1016/j.worlddev.2010.05.013

6. Looking to the future and useful tools for leveraging GVCs

Keywords: automation; digital transition; green transition; data; climate change; sustainability; global value chains; COVID

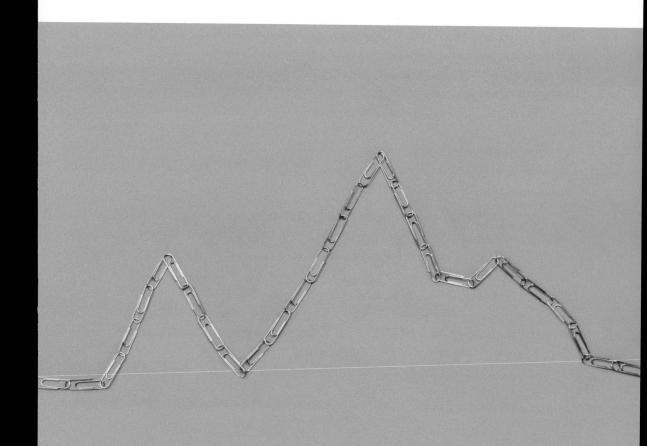

The economic and public health challenges and policy responses created by Covid-19 have led to an acceleration of some key pre-existing trends, namely geopolitical fragmentation, the reorganisation of GVCs and the adoption of new technologies. Economic recovery from Covid-19 has proven slower and more challenging than initially envisaged by many. The economic impact of conflict in Ukraine is also likely to take a significant toll on global growth and employment prospects. Moreover, while there are changing power relationships between MNEs and government partners, the former continue to enjoy considerable power and influence over GVCs.[1] All these shifts have profound implications for patterns of economic growth and prosperity at the national and regional levels.

As a result, the **public policy space remains fundamentally different from the past**. Additionally, there are new overarching policy targets, with digital and green transitions being top priorities. This fundamental shift in the public policy paradigm is a landmark feature of "recovery plans" the world over. The European Union's (EU) Recovery Plan is mobilising €750 billion through Next Generation EU, together with a reinforced long-term EU budget (2021–27) of €1100 billion. In the United States, the federal fiscal response has been estimated to be a record US$5.2 trillion, and the African Union is similarly mobilising resources around a 2021–27 Green Recovery Action Plan. In this renewed policy context, regional policies for international connectivity, GVCs and foreign direct investment (FDI) need to be thought out creatively.

Regional Studies Policy Impact Books
https://doi.org/10.1080/2578711X.2022.2099176

Firms cannot recover, build resilience or chart the sustainable future alone[2]—they need public sector engagement. **Together, private enterprise and policy decision-makers can seek new pathways for regional development and recovery at the intersection between global opportunities and local recovery.**

The selection of the most appropriate regional policy tools should be driven by solid evidence on what works in practice, when and under what conditions. Ideology and anecdotal evidence—often based on carefully selected cases of success—should be replaced by robust insights on effectiveness and impact. The approach needs to be holistic: **public policies should be considered as a coordinated portfolio of actions aimed at addressing different aspects of innovation in a global environment in constant evolution.** Pro-recovery policy tools focusing on "digital" and "green" priorities might be intrinsically "exclusive" in terms of their beneficiaries due to their complexity and managerial challenges.

Regions need tools that work in practice in order to support their search for new markets, innovation opportunities and upgrading patterns. For example, the 2021–27 Cohesion Policy includes new dedicated instruments specifically focused on GVCs in order to foster the ability of EU regions to build, embed and—ideally—reshape European value chains. With this new set of objectives, resources and tools, regional policies—in all their forms—are asked to contribute to a green and digital future for all territories. In the UK, the White Paper outlining the government's strategy for the "Levelling Up" of the economy also makes some reference to the importance of FDI and trade in shaping the developmental prospects of regions in decline after Brexit and Covid-19.[3] However, the knowledge base to support this new generation of "internationally open" regional policies remains limited, as has been extensively discussed in this book.

This book offers policymakers a set of tools that work in practice by **delivering concrete evidence-based answers to the pressing needs of people on the ground**, and by supporting the generation of new economic opportunities in all regions. Impactful local policies matter well beyond the economy, given their impacts on political behaviour and support for international cooperation and integration.[4]

The policy framework developed combines theoretical and empirical messages to deal with GVCs of today at the national and—especially—regional levels. However, all aspects of GVCs discussed in this book—building, embedding and reshaping—will likely continue to evolve in the future under the pressure of flux in the wider economic and policy environment. Policy decision-makers must plan for this uncertainty, and the following sections sketch some of the possibilities for change. The first section will discuss changes in the technological domain (in some cases accelerated by the pandemic and the digital transition). The second section will cover environmental domains. The third section briefly highlights some key issues and trends regarding the future of data and (regional) intelligence for FDI and GVC as something policy decision-makers should keep an eye on when incorporating this book's insights into the policy cycle.

6.1 GVCS AND THE DIGITAL TRANSITION: AUTOMATION, ARTIFICIAL INTELLIGENCE AND DIGITAL WORK PRACTICES

The policy domain is increasingly focused on the issues surrounding the Fourth Industrial Revolution, Industry 4.0, and the impact of work-from-home patterns. While the evidence on effects is limited, dialogue is widespread. There will be consequences for GVCs and the knowledge they can provide. Some feel they will likely boost GVCs as trade and communication costs reduce and new products are developed. Others see much changing for GVCs, with specific challenges in regions whose comparative advantage lies in the abundance of low-cost workers.[5] So it is cautious, pragmatic engagement with GVCs that should be taken. There are particular challenges and opportunities associated with building, embedding and reshaping, particularly with regard to the future of work.

Changing location preferences

New technologies may be influencing the location of economic activities in new ways, including both production and research and development (R&D) centres. One such example is influencing the location decisions of the MNE. Conditions of low productivity and low forecasted growth rates in many developed economies have increased discussion about the Fourth Industrial Revolution, with a particular focus on how to further drive economic growth through AI and robotics.[6] In context of the GVC story, **it is useful to think about value-added across tasks and broader thinking in the new paradigm, as outlined above**.

Some expect that MNEs will have lower incentives to pursue lower labour costs abroad. Instead, they might locate production where automation may more easily occur, especially in response to the risk and uncertainty triggered by growing geopolitical fragmentation and tensions. By looking at automation of occupation, estimates suggest that about 47% of total US employment faces the risk of computerisation. This might affect the organisation of both domestic value chains and GVCs.[7] However, in the new paradigm, looking at automation of tasks, estimations show that only 9% of jobs in 21 Organisation for Economic Co-operation and Development (OECD) countries face computerisation.[8] In this perspective, the reorganisation of MNE activities along the value chain in response to new technologies seems less challenging for growth and jobs. Indeed, some propose that MNEs are well placed to handle and reduce many of these fragmentation risks because of cross-border business activities and emerging technologies.[9]

However, despite this 9% figure, spatial impacts may be different across regions. Less advanced regions typically pursue less sophisticated tasks. If automation displaces these less sophisticated tasks, then consequences are expected on some of the previously mentioned internal and external location drivers. The regions potentially affected are twofold:

- Those who previously competed with each other on low labour cost, high job count, low value-added production tasks—typically further away from the technological frontier.

- Those with high labour cost, very low job count (i.e., one individual overseeing a system of autonomous machines)—typically closer to the technological frontier.

These regions may soon find themselves competing for the same tasks. MNEs may now find themselves having to make FDI decisions between these areas. Geographically this might mean that peripheral (often rural) regions or areas "in industrial decline" suffer especially strongly. The automation competes disproportionately with their typical reliance on manufacturing and low-skilled services.[10] In contrast, these rural and more remote areas may also benefit most from the reduction of distance that autonomous vehicles or enhanced communication technology will likely bring.[11] Therefore, their analysis on how to leverage GVCs in the future of work is particularly critical.

Changing impacts through knowledge exchange

There is little evidence surrounding new technologies and how they will change understanding of the regional impacts of GVCs. Questions about whether increasing Industry 4.0 will see the reshoring of activities differently remain.

Many fear the rise of automation. Critically, robots explicitly take up a different part of the value chain. The very nature of automation lends itself to more standardised services and, therefore, jobs in specific locations. In this case, **as MNEs return to more innovative economies, the reshoring of certain activities may not lead to the reshoring of jobs**.

This changing composition of employment is likely to vary between countries. The 9% estimated job losses through automation previously mentioned varies by location.[12] In South Korea it is 6%, and this compares with 12% in Austria. **The underpinning message for regional policymakers and in the context of GVCs is the importance of regional upskilling**. The exposure to robots has different effects on wages depending on the skill level of the employee.[13] Rather than some workers losing their jobs, workers may only need to adjust their tasks. The diagnostic tool used previously can achieve this.

Another relevant and emerging discussion is about deep learning. There is strong evidence of the shifting importance of application-orientated learning research.[14] This is a movement away from routinised human R&D to that of predictive computer-driven algorithms. Although potentially rewarding for individual companies, the change might have a potentially distorting effect from a GVC and regional perspective. This effect may first warp the decisions regarding the reasons for an MNE outsourcing its R&D to another region. However, it may also inhibit the region's ability to capture knowledge spillovers fully.

This discussion relates to a final aspect on how new technologies might affect embeddedness around the labour market effects of knowledge spillovers. As discussed, these are one of the significant drivers of spillovers and the diffusion of knowledge from FDI, such as the process of workers moving from one firm to another and bringing new knowledge with them. Autonomous robots and the data-driven nature of Industry 4.0 may negate the ability for the human transfer of knowledge. There may be less labour market effects on knowledge diffusion. Preliminary studies highlight that **artificial intelligence may facilitate learning and the imitation of technologies used across firms, activities and tasks**.[15] Knowledge externalities may occur in a new form—something requiring further thought. **The effects of GVC links and their implication for innovation at the regional level may therefore change**.

What implications to reshape GVCs

Many of the reshaping vertical policies outlined are for the GVCs of today. However, the creation of value chains through new technologies with horizontal policies ready for change are also necessary. Regions need the institutional capacity and foresight to connect. An emphasis on tools for reskilling help set the ground for reshaping the GVCs of tomorrow. Lifelong-learning mechanisms, such as competence centres or centres of excellence, help ensure regional skills are ready to cope and work within new GVCs. As Industry 4.0 brings new value-capture opportunities, regional decision-makers must think about futureproofing their reshaping policies. They cannot promote or link with the unknown. Partnering with firms to help ensure reskilling is relevant and will help anticipate this future risk. New technologies also have the potential to destroy GVCs—connectivity creates vulnerability to both highs and lows. This integrated nature of GVCs means when crisis strikes, it reverberates sharply down the chain. **The potential for future technological turbulence further emphasises the necessity to view GVC engagement both through vertical engagement and horizontal readiness**.

6.2 GREEN GVCS AND THE GREEN TRANSITION

The future of GVCs is influenced by new environmental concerns, legislations and actions. Currently emissions from fuel combustion linked to international trade are close to 27% of global emissions. Countries and regions will want to understand carbon embedded in trade to prevent carbon leakage. Current evidence shows most of this carbon in trade is imported by higher income OECD countries, while lower income non-OECD countries export it.[16]

Yet, as the globe transitions to net zero emissions, **more goods and services will become inherently green, creating new and different "green" global value chains (GGVCs)**. It is the future of global trade. Policy decision-makers who engage with lead firms and leverage these changes will be able to develop new green micro-specialisms for regional development.

Increasing sustainability becomes part of building and upgrading these GGVCs, and this can potentially be achieved in three key ways.

Firstly, **by firms**—namely the lead firm desiring sustainability for trade. Lead firms in particular will be increasingly held accountable for the carbon emissions of their entire value chain.[17] They are important and powerful actors to leverage with a company's supply chain emissions estimated to be over five times larger than its direct or indirect emissions from its own production. **Lead firms can thus leverage size, scale and specialisation to encourage supply chains to be greener.** Consider evidence from a study of 108 countries over seven years finding that international trade encouraged the adoption of environmental standards, specifically in this case, ISO 14001. This voluntary standard was adopted by firms, especially exporting firms that did so at an increased rate if the importing countries and their firms had high levels of adoption of ISO 14001.[18] In spite of previous firms' compliance with environmental standards or pollution history, the adoption of positive standards permeated through the value chain. This is a good example of end-market upgrading with firms moving into more sophisticated markets requiring more demanding standards. Additionally, it highlights the continued future importance of lead firms' influence on organisational practices in GVC. It is one where expected and extended pressure for lead firms to move beyond narrow cost-based models of competition towards the promotion of more sustainable development will only increase the greening of GVCs through, for example, corporate social responsibility recommendations.[19] Their global reach is also considerable, with lead firms exercising governance and strengthening control over standards and procedures along the value chain, driving efficiency improvements, which in turn has consequences in many geographies.[20]

Secondly, **by markets**, with **GVCs leading to potential competition on environmental standards**. In agriculture, Thailand hopes to move up the knowledge value chain by functional upgrading and chain/intersectoral upgrading. **This upgrading is explicitly leveraging GGVCs**. Policy decision-makers understood their current position on the chain and estimated bio-economy—the use or renewable biological resources—would generate 8–11% value-add when compared with 7% in traditional agricultural tasks.[21] The country has explicitly linked this industrial development with certain parts of the country making food-related industrial zones. These zones will help upskill citizens and provided value-added in food.

Thirdly, **by governments** with frameworks and legislation. For example, in March 2021, Germany's government approved proposals will require companies operating supply chains to enforce specific human rights and environmental standards. This represents one way that new sustainability standards will be necessary for MNEs and local suppliers. Softer public policy is currently leveraged in Cambodia where they have designed a specific supplier database for sustainable investment. Similarly, Ghana now has a special recognised category for sustainable investment. **This recognition sees a "green channel" of unique government engagement pre-investment and a "green (red) carpet" for aftercare**.[22]

The combination of these fundamental forces towards GGVCs has the potential to affect the geography of GVCs more generally. They will change the locational advantages of countries and regions, shaping impacts and influencing public policy. One example is regions building GVCs through clean energy, which will enjoy a new competitive advantage. Manufacturing is one such area. Currently countries such as China, Russia, Viet Nam, India and South Africa all have twice the carbon intensity embodied in international trade than the world average,[23] and will thus become less competitive in the shift to GGVCs. One specific GVC example is with energy-intensive production activities, such as steel, with these in future expected to be located closer to renewable energy sources. In Sweden this is occurring at a regional level, with Norrland, an area highly endowed with hydropower and proximity to iron ore,[24] developing new green micro-specialisms in steel. By electrolyzing water using hydropower electricity, green steel can be made eliminating 98% of the CO_2 normally released. Similarly, hydropower is being leveraged to make much more carbon-efficient batteries. Both these new GGVCs are driven by Swedish MNEs, Volvo, Scania and SSAB, the result of which is higher socio-economic growth in the region. Case study 6 looked at North Middle Sweden's IPAs and their focus on steel and advanced engineering, becoming potential facilitators of this change. Other steel-producing regions, such as Ruhr in Germany and Silesian Voivodeship in Poland, where the industry is mostly coal based and carbon intensive are at the risk of behind left behind.

While the direction of change for regions and their policies is still difficult to see with clarity, **the "greening" of GVCs needs to be carefully considered by regional policymakers**. At the same time, public policy oriented towards the green transition should carefully take into account the interconnected nature of regional economies and their impacts and implications for GVCs.

6.3 DATA AND INTELLIGENCE TO NAVIGATE CHANGE

Data limitations make it difficult to track the complex subnational geographies of GVCs and only allow for a high-level representation of the distribution of GVC stages globally. Databases such as UN COMTRADE, the World Input–Output database, OECD trade in value-added (TiVA) and fDi Markets (for greenfield FDI) are extensively leveraged in scholarly and policy work at the national and regional levels. However, data constraints become very significant when looking at subnational areas such as regions or cities. These can explain the limited evidence available to guide regional policies in the area of GVCs.

For example, at both the national and regional scales, FDI and foreign affiliates data need to be interpreted in a careful manner when it comes to the analysis of "buyer-driven" GVCs—where direct operations of MNEs and FDI play a different and often more limited role in explaining the geography of production. Furthermore, the position of regions in GVCs can be only indirectly captured by looking at establishment-level employment data when it is possible to access

https://doi.org/10.1080/2578711X.2022.2099176

information on firm (or ideally, establishment) and in particular on skill composition prox-ied, for example, through the distribution of employees across wage brackets. Additionally, the analysis of inwards foreign direct investment and outwards foreign direct investment flows across business function "re-organised" in GVC stages still cannot capture the degree of sophistication of products (or services) processed in a particular foreign establishment. Consider when looking at production-oriented FDI, how the geographical distribution of the production of high-end products differs from those of mass-produced goods. However, to the best of our knowledge, no systematic data link product-level information with firm ownership or internationalisation. This gap makes it impossible to address this important limitation for the analysis of the labour market impacts of GVC participation.

More generally, the measurement of GVCs is still an open issue and significant effort is needed to develop a coherent empirical portrait of GVCs, in particular when it comes to their sub-national geographies and the understanding of their wider impacts.[25] While the economic literature in this area is progressing significantly, a sound basis to inform regional and urban development policies remains limited.

Promising improvements come from the use of inter-country input–output (ICIO) tables that link production processes within and across countries to measure TiVA and participation in GVCs. The ICIO tables are a useful tool, representing domestic transaction flows of intermedi-ate goods and services across countries and inter-country flows of intermediates via exports and imports. Described as "one of the most useful tools for studying international production networks",[26] the detailed information provides beneficial insight. The OECD's TiVA initiative addresses the issue of the ill-capture of global production in conventional measures of inter-national trade. It does so by considering the value added by each country in the production of goods and services consumed globally. The TiVA database also includes indicators designed to inform policymakers better. The provision of new insights in relations between commerce and nations can take place, which is useful for both economic and environmental analysis.[27] These insights are particularly useful for an empirical painting of the GVC picture.[28]

6.4 FINAL REMARKS

The approach—one of leveraging variation and reflecting regional specificities to maxi-mise productivity-enhancing investment—is not new.[29] However, the tools to achieve this are. Recently in 2016, surveys highlighting development policy priorities saw an absence of FDI.[30] However, enhancing competitiveness and reducing regional inequalities were recur-ring objectives. These objectives are something this policy framework and the correct lever-aging of investment flows has considerable potential to encourage upgrading and regional development.

Work still needs to be done regarding this approach, especially in understanding what variation at both firm and locational levels is useful for decision-makers to draw regionally specific lessons from. The continuation of this study for subnational policies is vital. However, this book makes a positive start, and highlights several approaches available to regional policy decision-makers to help build, embed and reshape GVCs. There are still gaps that need filling, however, progress is underway and more resources are becoming available to enhance our understanding of GVCs.[31]

In its construction, this book has hopefully helped frame GVCs and development consequences for regions. It provides a useful, empirically grounded policy framework of leveraging GVCs through building, embedding and reshaping for regional upgrading. Highlighted throughout are its six key messages detailed in the beginning: (1) the key to connectivity and with (2) all GVCs being different, seeing (3) regions developing fine-grained specialisms on tasks being beneficial. To account for firm and location variation, (4) building institutional and informational bridges help, as does (5) leveraging linkages to ensure positive impact. The (6) proactive pursuit of knowledge and active internationalisation shows their merits. With its small contribution, regional policy decision-makers now have better resources with which to take action on "not only a matter of whether to participate in the global economy, but how to do so gainfully."[32]

NOTES

1 Ghauri P, Strange R and Cooke FL (2021) Research on international business: The new realities. *International Business Review*, 30(2): 101794. https://doi.org/10.1016/j.ibusrev.2021.101794.

2 Strange R (2022) The future of global value chains: Key issues. *Columbia FDI Perspectives*, 328.

3 Bailey D, Crescenzi R, Roller E, Anguelovski I, Datta A and Harrison J (2021) Regions in Covid-19 recovery. *Regional Studies*, 55(12): 1955–1965. doi:10.1080/00343404.2021.2003768.

4 Crescenzi, R, Di Cataldo, M, Giua, M (2020) It's not about the money. EU funds, local opportunities, and Euroscepticism *Regional Science and Urban Economics*, 84, 103556.

5 World Bank. (2020) *World Development Report 2020: Trading for Development in the Age of Global Value Chains*. Washington, DC: World Bank. https://www.worldbank.org/en/publication/wdr2020

6 Morikawa M (2017) Firms' expectations about the impact of AI and robotics: Evidence from a survey. *Economic Inquiry*, 55(2): 1054–1063. doi:10.1111/ecin.12412.

7 Frey CB and Osborne MA (2017) The future of employment: How susceptible are jobs to computerisation? *Technological Forecasting and Social Change*, 114: 254–280.

8 Arntz M, Gregory T and Zierahn U (2016) *The Risk of Automation in Jobs in OECD Countries: A Comparative Analysis* (Science, Employment and Migration Working Paper No. 189). OECD Publ.

9 Contractor FJ (2022) The world economy will need even more globalization in the post-pandemic 2021 decade. *Journal of International Business Studies*, 53(1): 156–171. doi:10.1057/s41267-020-00394-y.

10 OECD (2019) *OECD Regional Outlook 2019: Leveraging Megatrends for Cities and Rural Areas*. Paris: OECD Publ.

11 OECD (2019) *Regions in Industrial Transition: Policies for People and Places*. Paris: OECD Publ.

12 Arntz et al. (2016), see Reference 7.

13 Dauth W, Findeisen S, Südekum J and Woessner N (2017) German robots—the impact of industrial robots on workers. CEPR Discussion Paper No. DP12306. https://ssrn.com/abstract=3039031

14 Cockburn IM, Henderson R and Stern S (2018) *The Impact of Artificial Intelligence on Innovation*. Cambridge, MA: National Bureau of Economic Research (NBER).

15 Aghion P, Jones BF and Jones CI (2017) *Artificial Intelligence and Economic Growth*. Cambridge, MA: National Bureau of Economic Research (NBER). doi: 10.3386/w23928

16 Yamano N and Guilhoto J (2020) *CO$_2$ Emissions Embodied in International Trade and Domestic Final Demand: Methodology and Results using the OECD Inter-Country Input–Output Database* (Science, Technology and Industry Working Papers No. 2020/11). Paris: OECD Publ. https://doi.org/10.1787/8f2963b8-en.

17 Asian Infrastructure Investment Bank (2021) *Sustaining Global Value Chains. Asian Infrastructure Finance 2021*. https://www.aiib.org/en/news-events/asian-infrastructure-finance/2021/_common/pdf/AIIB-Asian-Infrastructure-Finance-2021.pdf

18 Prakash A and Potoski M (2006) Racing to the bottom? Trade, environmental governance, and ISO 14001. *American Journal of Political Science*, 50(2): 350–364.

19 Gereffi G and Lee J (2016) Economic and social upgrading in global value chains and industrial clusters: Why governance matters. *Journal of Business Ethics*, 133(1): 25–38. doi:10.1007/s10551-014-2373-7.

20 Baldwin R (2016) *The Great Convergence: Information Technology and the New Globalisation*. Cambridge, MA: Harvard University Press.

21 Sirisup T (2021) Executive Director, International Affairs Bureau, Thailand Board of Investment Forum on sustainable investment in ASEAN, online.

22 For more information on GGVCs in Africa, see Colenbrander S, Harman O, Tshukudu K and Venables A (Forthcoming 2022) *Positioning Emerging African Cities for a Green Growth Transition* (Growth Brief). IGC.

23 Using data from Yamano and Guilhoto (2020), see Reference 15.

24 *The Economist*. (2021) Green steel. *The Economist*, 439: 29–30.

25 Johnson RC (2018) Measuring global value chains. *Annual Review of Economics*, 10(1): 207–236. doi:10.1146/annurev-economics-080217-053600.

26 Meng B and Yamano N (2017) Compilation of a regionally extended inter-country input–output table and its application to global value chain analyses. *Journal of Economic Structures*, 6(1): 23.

27 Miller RE and Blair PD (2009) *Input–Output Analysis: Foundations and Extensions*. Cambridge: Cambridge University Press; Murray J and Wood R (2010) *The Sustainability Practitioner's Guide to Input–Output Analysis*. Champaign, IL: Common Ground .

28 WTO–IDE (2011) *Trade Patterns and Global Value Chains in East Asia: From Trade in Goods to Trade in Tasks*. Geneva: World Trade Organisation (WTO). https://www.wto.org/english/res_e/booksp_e/ stat_tradepat_globvalchains_e.pdf; OECD–WTO (2013) *Measuring Trade in Value Added: An OECD– WTO Joint Initiative*. https://www.oecd.org/industry/ind/measuring-trade-in-value-added.htm.; OECD–WTO–World Bank Group (2014) Global value chains: Challenges, opportunities, and implications for policy. In *Report Prepared for Submission to the G20 Trade Ministers Meeting*. https://www. oecd.org/g20/topics/trade-and-investment/gvc_report_g20_july_2014.pdf; Koopman R, Wang Z and Wei S-J (2014) Tracing value-added and double counting in gross exports. *American Economic Review*, 104(2): 459–494; Meng and Yamano (2017), see Reference 25.

29 OECD (2011) *OECD Regional Outlook 2011: Building Resilient Regions for Stronger Economies*. Paris: OECD Publ. https://www.oecd-ilibrary.org/urban-rural-and-regional-development/ oecd-regional-outlook-2011_9789264120983-en

30 OECD (2016) *OECD Regional Outlook 2016: Productive Regions for Inclusive Societies*. Paris: OECD Publ. https://www.oecd.org/regional/oecd-regional-outlook-2016-9789264260245-en.htm

31 Crescenzi R and Harman O (2022) *Climbing Up Global Value Chains: Leveraging FDI for Economic Development* (Report). Singapore: Hinrich Foundation. https://www.hinrichfoundation.com/ research/wp/fdi/global-value-chains-gvc-foreign-direct-investment-fdi-economic-development/.

32 Gereffi G and Fernandez-Stark K (2016) *Global Value Chain Analysis: A Primer*. Durham, NC: Duke University. http://hdl.handle.net/10161/12488.

https://doi.org/10.1080/2578711X.2022.2099176